DIGITAL
MOVIEMAKING

KNACK

DIGITAL MOVIEMAKING

Tools & Techniques to Make Movies like a Pro

Tyler Cullen

Photographs by Eric Westpheling

Guilford, Connecticut
An imprint of Globe Pequot Press

To buy books in quantity for corporate use
or incentives, call **(800) 962-0973**
or e-mail **premiums@GlobePequot.com**.

Editorial Director: Cynthia Hughes
Editor: Katie Benoit
Project Editor: Tracee Williams
Cover Design: Paul Beatrice, Bret Kerr
Interior Design: Paul Beatrice
Layout: Maggie Peterson and Melissa Evarts
Cover Photos by: Eric Westpheling
Interior Photos by: Eric Westpheling with the exception of those listed on pages 234–35.
Movie Poster Graphics by: Lauren Panepinto, www.laurenpanepinto.com

Library of Congress Cataloging-in-Publication Data

Cullen, Tyler.
  Knack digital moviemaking : tools & techniques to make movies like a pro / Tyler Cullen ; photographs by Eric Westpheling.
    p. cm.
  Includes index.
  ISBN 978-1-59921-991-2
  1. Digital cinematography. I. Title. II. Title: Digital moviemaking.
  TR860.C85 2010
  778.5'3—dc22
                                        2010021234

Dedication

To my Dad, for the unwavering support through the years.

Acknowledgments

Special thanks to Cynthia Hughes, Katie Benoit, and Tracee Williams for helping me through the process of writing this book. Thanks to Eric Westpheling for filling these pages with great photos. Thanks to my sister, friends, and roommates for listening to my ideas and rants. Thanks to you for reading this book, may you make truly awesome films.

Photographer Acknowledgments

I'd like to thank the wonderful staff at Knack Books, especially Katie Benoit and Tracee Williams. Much gratitude also goes to David Cohen and George Alvarez for their assistance with this project. And lastly, as always, I'd like to thank Anne Watters, my fiancée, for her unwavering love and assistance, and for being a very patient model.

CONTENTS

INTRODUCTION

It wasn't long after getting my first camcorder and computer that I began making my own videos. Over the years, I became obsessed with learning ways to make my videos both more professional and more fun to watch for my friends and family. My first videos were simple music videos and slideshows, but the more I learned about the improving technology, the more watchable my videos became and the more I enjoyed making them.

I wanted to learn everything I could about filmmaking, from start to finish. I started reading books on everything from writing screenplays to directing to sound design. With a firm understanding of the technical side of movie-making, I started watching movies differently. Instead of just watching movies for the story or entertainment value, I observed how the movies were constructed from the inside out. To this day, I still enjoy watching movies more the second time around than I do the first time because that second viewing allows me to focus on the production values of the film without getting lost in the story.

Opening the doors of film-making to a wider community

While many young filmmakers of the past persevered through technological restraints to make films on 16mm film and other formats, others didn't have the means to buy equipment or the motivation to make films when it was

so much harder to get started. Many of today's filmmakers gain considerable experience at a very young age and have a wide variety of digital equipment available to them. There are four distinct developments worth mentioning that have made filmmaking much more accessible to the masses within the past decade:

First, video editing software is much more accessible to the general public. All new computers have video editing software included as part of the software package. Film-makers no longer have to have a suite of iMacs or spend thousands of dollars to build their own computer editing stations. The software continues to get easier to use for beginning editors while also allowing for more experienced users to apply advanced effects that could only be executed by large movie studios just a decade ago.

Secondly, digital video has become widely available and easy to produce. More importantly, the cost of digital cameras and camcorders has come down significantly. With the move away from traditional film, production costs have decreased, opening up the world of filmmaking to a whole new demographic. In today's digital savvy world, most people own at least one device that is able to record video, whether it is a phone, a digital camera, or a camcorder. And DV cameras, with their tolerance for lighting variables and their digital sound recording capabilities, provide movie-makers with a very forgiving tool for capturing stories.

Thirdly, although digital video files are very big, most home computers now have the hard drives and processors necessary to cope with them. In addition, portable storage devices like USB memory sticks allow users to move big files between computers very easily.

Finally, improved and faster broadband Internet connections allow the average person to view and share DV files with ease.

These advances in technology have not only enabled young filmmakers to learn the language of film much faster and with ease, they have also opened the doors of filmmaking to a much wider, younger, more digital-savvy community. If you have access to a digital video camera and a computer, you can produce professional-quality work. You don't need a lot of cash and you don't need to know the right people. All you need is a great story, a certain amount of technical skill, and the drive and determination to realize your vision.

So why should you read this book?

If you have a digital camcorder, or you're thinking of purchasing one and want to improve the quality of your edited video projects, you should read this book. You'll find tips, techniques, and advice that will go a long way toward making the work you do behind the camera and in your editing software look more professional and be more dynamic. Or, perhaps you're thinking of making your first short film or low-budget film. *Knack Digital Moviemaking* will help you in all aspects of its creation, from start to finish.

Most of the techniques shown in this book are easy to learn and can go a long way in making your videos better. Many first-time filmmakers are quick to find out that their videos might not live up to their original vision. This is often because beginning filmmakers do not know the basic techniques and skills to bring their movies to the next level. Remember, it may be easier to create, edit, and share a video than ever, but that doesn't mean that it's easier to create, edit, and share a *good* video. It still takes the same amount of skill and know-how to produce great work. In fact, it may be even harder now due to the increased competition in this ever-growing field.

Still, if you are truly devoted to making great movies, this book is only a beginning. Entire books could be, and have been, written on each chapter of this book. Look at *Knack*

Digital Moviemaking as a starting point for your educational journey. After you have read this book, you may find that screenwriting interests you more than cinematography, or that editing interests you more than sound. The field of filmmaking and digital video is always changing and the best filmmakers are willing to keep learning as the times and technology continue to evolve.

This book can be read from beginning to end or you can jump around from chapter to chapter, spread to spread, depending on your interests. And remember, you can learn a lot by reading, but you'll also learn a lot by doing. Regardless of your experience, quality of equipment, or level of skill, I encourage you to pick up your camera and get out there and start shooting. And remember to have fun.

HISTORY OF FILMMAKING

From the late nineteenth century till the present, film has come a long way

The very first motion picture was filmed in 1878 using a series of twenty-four cameras to photograph a horse named Sallie Gardner as she galloped on a track. Most motion pictures were a novelty at this time, but the coming years would see movies develop into an established large-scale entertainment industry.

During the 1920s, sound recording devices were invented and ushered in a new era of film with synchronous sound. What followed was the Golden Age of film. During this time, eight studios collectively produced 95 percent of all American films.

The rise of independent movie producers and exhibitors

Hollywood

- In the early 1900s motion picture production companies moved from New York and New Jersey to California to take advantage of the better weather, especially the abundance of sunshine.

- The city of Hollywood came to be so strongly associated with the film industry that the word "Hollywood" became synonymous with the entire American film industry.

- The famous Hollywood sign that we know today originally read as "Hollywoodland." It was erected in 1923 to advertise a new housing development.

Silent Era

- The pre-1930s era of film is referred to as the Silent Era of film. Films produced during this time had no synchronized recorded sound or spoken dialogue.

- Title cards, muted gestures, and body movement were used to communicate acting and dialogue in silent films.

- To compensate, the visual quality of the movies in this era was often extremely high.

- A musical instrument almost always accompanied silent film screenings, the most common being a single piano.

along with the rise of television in the 1950s eventually led to the fall of the studio system. The '50s and '60s saw a large number of musicals, historical movies, and other films take advantage of the larger screens, wider framing, and increased sound quality. By the late 1960s, audience numbers were dwindling at an alarming rate. The studios did not know how to reach the youth market. By the time the baby boomer generation was coming of age in the 1960s and 1970s, Old Hollywood was losing money hand over fist.

To combat the loss in viewer numbers, the studios moved away from a producer-driven system that gave directors little creative control and started hiring young filmmakers, who were allowed to make their films with relatively little studio control. This group of young filmmakers briefly changed the business from the producer-driven Hollywood system of the past to a more director-driven system.

This setup would once again flip-flop back to the producers' control when high-concept, moneymaking blockbusters like *Jaws* and *Star Wars* became box-office hits in the mid to late '70s.

Hollywood Golden Age

- The release of *The Jazz Singer* in 1927 marked the end of the Silent Era and the beginning of the Golden Age of Hollywood. It was the first feature-length motion picture with synchronized dialogue sequences.

- Films of the Golden Age were often genre films that stuck to a particular formula.

- *The Wizard of Oz, Gone with the Wind, Casablanca, It's a Wonderful Life, King Kong, City Lights,* and *Citizen Kane* are just some of the classics that were released during this period.

New Hollywood

- "New Hollywood" refers to the time from the mid-1960s to the early 1980s.

- *Bonnie and Clyde,* released in 1967, was one of the first and most significant movies in the New Hollywood era. It featured a mix of graphic violence, sex, and humor that broke the mold of the typical Hollywood product.

- Other landmark films from this era included *The Graduate, Easy Rider, The French Connection, Raging Bull, Taxi Driver, The Godfather, 2001: A Space Odyssey,* and *Annie Hall.*

STUDIO VERSUS INDEPENDENT
Studio and independent films differ in many ways

Money is the key element that separates a studio film from an independent film. Studio films secure a variety of funding sources that make their productions possible. Funding can come from private investors, film production studios, presales, product placements, or a combination of sources. Studio films also tend to use famous actors, directors, and Hollywood production companies that make these projects attractive to investors. Independent films rarely secure funding using the same methods as productions supported by major Hollywood studios. Not having a major star to help sell the film is the main reason why independent films find it difficult to get funded. Many independent film directors or producers fund these projects using their own money because they have limited resources for film production money.

Hollywood's Studio System

- Hollywood's major production companies have gradually transformed into management companies that put together artistic teams on a project-by-project basis and distribute the finished products.

- On average, only one in every six films produced results in bottom line profit. However, the major blockbusters take in much more than their production cost and end up paying for less successful films.

- Most Hollywood films don't begin to make a profit until they move to TV, DVD, pay-TV, and foreign distribution.

The Sundance Film Festival

- The Sundance Film Festival is the largest independent festival in the United States. It takes place annually in Park City, Utah.

- Beginning as a low-profile venue for small budget independent filmmakers, the festival has grown into the premier showcase for independent film.

- Many filmmakers got their start from showing films at Sundance, including Kevin Smith, Robert Rodriguez, Quentin Tarantino, and Steven Soderbergh.

Many studio films have an advantage over independent film projects when it comes to the production stage, as well. Production teams working on a studio film have access to remote locations, elaborate set designs, and visual effects that help add visual appeal to their projects.

Equipment expenses alone could potentially bankrupt an independent film before production even starts. Many independent films have simple locations and minimal effects or stunts. Filmmakers who produce these projects usually rely on donated goods, services, and locations, which limit the options for production elements.

Studio films are often produced by companies that also own a distribution company, thus providing an automatic sales outlet that helps studio films make their production budget money back plus profits.

Independent filmmakers submit their projects to film festivals and markets to attract distribution offers from larger studios. While thousands of independent films are submitted to festivals each year, only a few get accepted, and an even smaller percentage gets sold.

Indiewood

- The 1990s saw a convergence of traditional independent films and Hollywood. Following the success of *Pulp Fiction* in 1994, Hollywood studios opened subsidiary studios focusing on indie films, allowing them to cash in on the independent film movement.

- Some of the most successful independent films in recent years are hybrids between the traditional independent films and studio films, called "Indiewood" films. These Indiewood movies typically include larger budgets, bigger stars, and increased spending on marketing.

Advantages of Independent Film

- Indie films allow the artist to circumvent excessive studio control on their projects.

- When you finance independently the creative control remains a little more within your grasp: actors can step outside typical typecast roles; directors can craft their own unique vision; and writers can often see their scripted vision through the entire development process.

- The independent film world is far from utopia, but it definitely has its advantages.

PAST CAMERAS
The digital revolution has come a long way from its simple camera roots

The use of film, video, and digital video in cameras has evolved extensively in the last century. Once only reserved for the extremely wealthy, today everyone has the ability to record video.

Before the video camera became popular for home use in the 1970s and 80s, home movies were made using 8mm and 16mm film formats. Average consumers preferred the smaller gauge of the 8mm film, while more professional videographers opted for 16mm.

The increased popularity of television after the 1950s sparked an evolution in home movies. During the 1970s and 1980s, television stations switched from recording on film to videotape. It

KNACK DIGITAL MOVIEMAKING

35mm Film

- 35mm film is the type of film gauge most commonly used for both still photography and motion pictures. It has remained relatively unchanged since its introduction in 1892.

- 35mm film is the standard by which all video formats are judged.

- The introduction and wide use of digital video has not killed 35mm film. While digital cinema is becoming more and more popular, 35mm is still the most popular format used for Hollywood movies.

16mm Film

- 16mm film is a popular type of film used for motion pictures and nontheatrical filmmaking.

- It was introduced in 1923 as an inexpensive amateur alternative to the conventional 35mm film.

- 16mm film cameras were used extensively in World War II and continued to develop in the post-war years.

- 16mm film has been used extensively in television, movies, and documentaries throughout the years.

was easier to work with, more affordable, and could be viewed immediately. Consumers followed soon after. Use of video camcorders and their accompanying VCR systems exploded in popularity during this time and continued into the early 1990s.

After that, since most consumers had previously used camcorders or worked on video, the transition to digital video was an easy, small step. The first mini-digital videocassettes appeared in the early 1990s, allowing camera manufacturers to create even smaller and higher-quality camcorders for consumer use.

8mm Film

- 8mm film is a film format where the filmstrip is eight millimeters wide. The two main versions are Standard 8 and Super 8.

- Standard 8 was developed by Kodak during the Great Depression and released on the market in 1932.

- Super 8 was released in 1965. Super 8 featured a better image quality and was easier to load and cartridge.

- Amateur filmmakers quickly adopted the format.

Early VHS Recorders

- The first portable video cameras were released In the late 1970s. These early units were big, bulky, and used a VCR with an attached camera.

- In 1982, the recorder and the camera were combined. These units became known as the camcorder (CAMera + reCORDER = camcorder).

- In 1985, the VHS-C was released, which allowed camera manufacturers to develop smaller camcorders.

GOING DIGITAL

Digital video has made it possible for any filmmaker to realize his cinematic vision

With a digital camcorder in hand, you can now make your very own professional-quality film at a fraction of the cost it takes to make a feature film with a traditional celluloid film camera. With no film reel needed, you avoid high processing costs, which can take up a large percentage of a small film's budget.

Panasonic and Sony introduced the first digital video cameras in 1995. These camcorders were small, light, and portable, and they produced better images than analog video. Along with digital video came new film features, such as inherent low-light recording capability and electronic image stabilization, features that eliminated the necessity for large camera crews typical of analog video production.

Digital Cinematography

- While most major motion pictures are still shot on film, digital cinematography has gained widespread acceptance over the last few years.

- Digital cinematography seems destined to eventually eclipse film-based

- acquisition, much as digital photo cameras have largely replaced film-based photo cameras in the still photography world.

- Digital video can also be edited on a personal computer that has the proper hardware and software.

Early Digital Camcorders

- In 1995, Panasonic and Sony introduced the first digital video cameras. It was an enormous milestone.

- These early digital camcorders used digital videotapes, such as the MiniDV.

- The high quality of DV images quickly gained favor with amateur filmmakers and mainstream broadcasters.

With the advent of digital video, editing became much easier; the video no longer had to be converted from an analog signal to digital data, as it was recorded digitally from the start. The FireWire offered a straightforward way to transfer that data without the need for additional hardware or compression. With this innovation, one could edit on standard computers with software-only packages. Digital video enabled real desktop editing that produced high-quality results at a fraction of the cost of other systems.

Camcorders Today

- The storage media, imaging, and audio capabilities have all improved as digital video technology has evolved.

- Most filmmaking schools have switched from 16mm film to digital video to reduce expenses and for the ease of editing digital video.

- If you compare today's digital camcorders' video with video taken twenty years ago, the evolution in quality is truly impressive.

Directors Going Digital

- For the last twenty-five years, many respected filmmakers like George Lucas have predicted that digital cinematography would bring about a revolution in filmmaking.

- Many high profile directors have embraced digital video technology. Slumdog Millionaire, The Curious Case of Benjamin Button, Superbad, Star Wars II and III, and Avatar were all shot digitally.

- Some directors such as Christopher Nolan, M. Night Shyamalan, and Paul Thomas Anderson have vowed to continue to only shoot on film.

HIGH DEFINITION
Forget film and standard definition—HD video is the future

After years of anticipation in the film industry, high-definition video has finally gone mainstream in professional video. HD video is now more popular and more inexpensive than standard definition (SD) was only a few years ago. Almost any video with a frame size greater than 576 lines tall is considered HD. HD video is generally either 1920 x 1080 or 1280 x 720, with a 16:9 aspect ratio. The aspect ratio of an image is

the ratio of the width of the image to its height, expressed as two numbers separated by a colon.

HD video for consumers has been around for about twenty years, even though it has only recently developed a sizable audience. In the early 1980s the Federal Communications Commission (FCC) set up the Advanced Television Systems Committee to define the specifications for HD broadcasts

High-definition Television

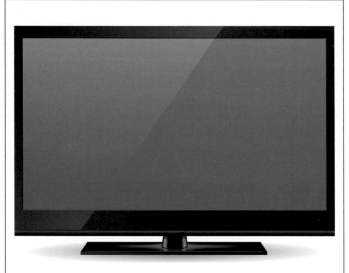

Standard-definition Television

- High definition is rapidly replacing standard definition when it comes to television broadcasts.

- Today the majority of televisions sold in the United States are HDTVs. To capitalize on this technology, try

to purchase high-definition televisions as opposed to standard-definition ones.

- New technologies come out every year, but nothing on the scale of the shift from standard-def to high-def TV will occur for a long time.

- Standard-definition television is based on 480 lines of vertical resolution and may have either 4:3 or 16:9 aspect ratios.

- While standard definition has not gone away completely, when compared to HD, its disadvantages are clear.

- Standard-definition programming is available in both widescreen and non-widescreen formats.

- Standard definition offers marginal video quality, but only uses a small amount of space when placed on storage media such as a hard drive or DVD.

such as resolution, frame rates, and aspect ratios. Broadcasters began HD broadcasts in 1996.

High-definition image sources include digital cable and satellite broadcast, high-definition disc (Blu-Ray), Internet downloads, and the latest generation of video game consoles. Most computers are capable of HD or higher resolutions over VGA, DVI, and/or HDMI cables. Storing and playing HD movies requires a disc that holds more information, like a Blu-Ray disc, the optical disc standard.

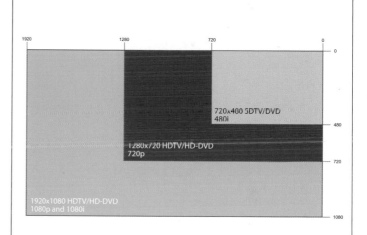
HD Video

- Take one look at the image on an HDTV compared to the image on an SDTV and you will see the dramatic difference in picture quality.

- HD video beats out SD video in every conceivable category, and with prices of these TVs decreasing every day, HD is also proving to be the best bang for your buck.

- HD video capture takes much more hard drive space than SD video, approximately five times as much.

HD versus SD

```
1920          1280         720              0
                                            0

                   720x480 SDTV/DVD
                   480i                     480

   1280x720 HDTV/HD-DVD
   720p                                     720

1920x1080 HDTV/HD-DVD
1080p and 1080i                            1080
```

- The chart above illustrates the relative sizes of different video formats and sizes with a count of total pixels.

- High-definition video has one or two million pixels per frame, roughly five times that of SD.

- There are many different types of HD, which we will explain in a later chapter.

3D & THE FUTURE
3D movies are experiencing a resurgence; here is what you should know

Three-dimensional film technology may seem like a brand new invention, but filmmakers have been experimenting with this type of film for a long time.

The first theatrical screenings of 3D test reels occurred in 1915 in New York City. The footage shown was of dancing girls and Niagara Falls. The 3D images were produced by using two film strips projected on top of one another, one using reds, the other greens. The film was then viewed using filtered glasses to decipher the image.

The early 3D film tests never caught on with audiences. Movie studios started experimenting with 3D films again in the early 1950s when television first started gaining

Cell Phone Camera

- Imagine a future where the cell phone you have in your pocket right now is capable of producing images that rival the video produced by today's high-definition camcorders.

- Granted, this technology is a ways off, but it is coming.

- Such technology will open up a new world of film-making, allowing people to shoot, edit, and distribute their films with their mobile devices.

- Even today there are online film festivals that specifi-cally showcase short films made with cell phones.

Digital Camera

- The digital photo cameras of today can take stunning pictures in addition to pro-ducing good video.

- Camera manufacturers will work to improve the video quality of these devices as demand increases.

- Having a hybrid device that can fit in your pocket and perform equally well when shooting video or taking pictures will open up many possibilities in the worlds of filmmaking and photography.

popularity. People flocked to movies like *Bwana Devil, House of Wax,* and *Creature from the Black Lagoon.* However, high cost and technical difficulties plagued 3D films from this era.

In the early 1980s, 3D cinema again experienced a brief resurgence, this time in part due to a decrease in box office sales because of the VCR. This round of 3D films included *Friday the 13th 3D, Jaws 3D,* and many others.

Although some might disagree, the 3D craze brought on by *Avatar* in 2009 seems to be more than just a passing fad. Major theater chains are acting quickly to expand the number of 3D theaters. Theaters offering 3D screenings are still a minority, however, so a 2D version of the film is almost always simultaneously released.

A well-made 3D movie can provide an audience with an unparalleled cinematic experience that stimulates the imagination in a way that is undeniable. The 3D photography uses special cameras to record two perspectives (left eye and right eye) to create the depth illusion of a three-dimensional image. Making a 3D movie requires a completely new workflow system at every level, from scriptwriting to post-production.

3D Movies

- With the financial success of *Avatar,* movie studios will continue to produce more and more 3D movies.

- Movies that were originally shot in two dimensions will be converted to 3D and re-released to capitalize on the 3D trend.

- 3D digital technology is still in its infancy. As it continues to grow and evolve, we will see movies with more immersion and impressive three-dimensional graphics.

- DVDs, video games, and television will all experiment with 3D technology in the future.

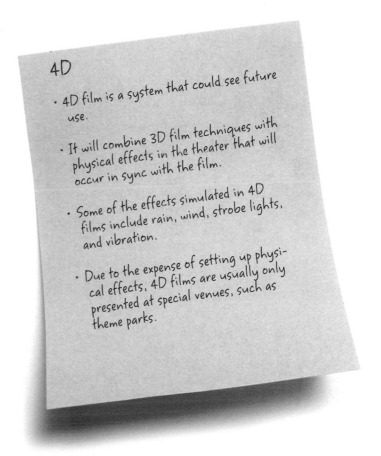

4D

- 4D film is a system that could see future use.

- It will combine 3D film techniques with physical effects in the theater that will occur in sync with the film.

- Some of the effects simulated in 4D films include rain, wind, strobe lights, and vibration.

- Due to the expense of setting up physical effects, 4D films are usually only presented at special venues, such as theme parks.

11

AUDIENCE
Try to understand everything you can about your audience

One of the first things you need to ask yourself before you set out to make any film is, "Who would be interested in watching this?" Sometimes we filmmakers get so caught up in the making of a video that we forget that someone else has to watch it. We tend to assume that just because we enjoy making videos, others will enjoy watching them. You can make a video that to you is a masterpiece, but that masterpiece may go completely unappreciated by the audience.

Spend time learning about your target audience so you can keep their needs in the forefront of your mind while writing your script. The key to success as a video maker is to know who is likely to watch your video and to then produce the video specifically for that group.

Let's say you wanted to make a short video about how to

Captivating Your Audience

- Before you start production on your film, consider how and where the audience will be watching it.

- The movie theater produces the most captive audiences.

- An audience watching a DVD or TV at home is less captive. If your film doesn't hook them they can simply change the channel or turn off the DVD.

- The audience watching streaming video online is by far the least captive. You only have seconds to hook them before they click away to something else.

Young Audiences

- Teenagers tend to favor movies with a lot of action and fast cutting.

- Young people have a shorter attention span but they can process and interpret quick editing better than older audiences.

- You can pack lots of information into documentaries made for younger audiences as long as the subject matter is shown in an entertaining way.

- The pace of movies has gotten progressively faster as more young people have been raised on music videos and Internet clips.

ride a bike. While any how-to video about bike riding will contain similar details, a video made for little kids will look and sound much different than one made for adults.

It can be said that there are three distinct purposes for any video you will make: to inform, to instruct, or to entertain. The goal of the nightly news program is to inform; a cooking show to instruct; and sitcoms to entertain. Some videos will fall into multiple categories, but anything you tape will fall into at least one. Keep these categories in mind as you move forward with the production of your film.

Older Audiences

- Older people may have trouble keeping up with the pace of movies made for younger audiences.

- Because they have a lifetime of movie watching behind them and expect certain things to happen, older audiences may be less open to experimentation.

- Use common sense: A video made for an older audience shouldn't include slang and subject matter that they are not familiar with.

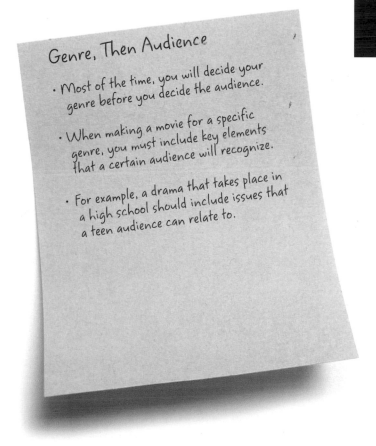

Genre, Then Audience

- Most of the time, you will decide your genre before you decide the audience.

- When making a movie for a specific genre, you must include key elements that a certain audience will recognize.

- For example, a drama that takes place in a high school should include issues that a teen audience can relate to.

NARRATIVE
The most common type of film, it tells a fictional story meant to entertain

The narrative is a type of film that tells a story using the production elements of camera, sound, editing, lighting, acting, visual composition, and effects combined with story elements of character, setting, plot, cause and effect, and time structure. Narrative films have been the most popular types of films since the early twentieth century. When you think of "the movies," you are most often thinking of narrative films.

Continuity editing is the dominant style of editing used in film narratives. Films are edited to suggest a progression of events in a logical way, which allows the audience to lose themselves in the fiction that unfolds onscreen.

Narrative films fall into different genres or subgenres. A

Drama

- A drama film is a film genre that depends mostly on in-depth development of realistic characters dealing with emotional themes.

- All film genres can include dramatic elements, but typically, films considered drama films focus mainly on the drama of the main issue.

- Drama films have been nominated for the Academy Award more than any other film genre.

Comedy

- Comedy film is a genre of film in which the main emphasis is on humor. Comedies are light-hearted dramas, made to amuse, entertain, and provide enjoyment.

- Comedies usually come in two general formats: comedian-led and situation-comedies that are told within a narrative.

- They come in many forms and subgenres such as musical-comedy, romantic comedy, slapstick, parody, gross-out, and screwball.

- Comedy films typically have a happy ending.

genre is a type of film with recognizable plots, locations, subject matter, and techniques. If your goal is to make a genre film, you must know the components of the genre that your film will fit into. You need to know the genre rules and your audience's understanding of them before you decide if you want to replicate or reject them.

Dramas are the largest genre, with a wide variety of subgenres housed under this category. Dramas are serious films that portray realistic characters, settings, situations, and stories.

Comedies are meant to make you laugh. They tend to be audience-specific because what you may find funny, somebody else may not. Comedies have many subgenres such as romantic, slapstick, parody, and dark.

Action and adventure movies are full of fight scenes, gun battles, car chases, stunts, disasters, and explosions that are meant to excite your audience. Horror movies entertain viewers by scaring them and placing them in frightening situations. Thrillers and suspense films combine elements with other genres such as action, crime, and horror to keep the audience on the edge of their seats throughout the movie.

Action

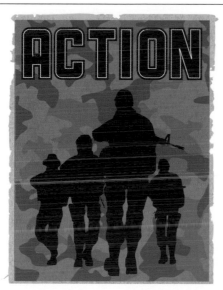

- Action film is a film genre wherein the story is largely told through physical action as opposed to dialogue.

- While action films are often box-office hits, relatively few action films receive critical praise.

- They almost always have a hero or heroine struggling against incredible odds, life-threatening circumstances, or an evil villain.

- Action films have traditionally been aimed at male audiences.

Horror

- Horror films are movies that are meant to elicit the emotions of fear, horror, and terror from the audience.

- Horror films have been dismissed as violent, low budget B movies but all major studios and many famous directors have made films that fall into this genre.

- Many horror films incorporate elements of other genres such as science fiction, fantasy, thriller, and even comedy.

DOCUMENTARY

A documentary's central goal is to tell a realistic and true story

A documentary film is a movie that attempts in some way to document reality. Its goal is not to tell a fictional story but essentially to tell a realistic and true story by presenting facts and interviews. The scenes are carefully chosen and arranged but they are not scripted, and the people in a documentary film are not actors. Some documentary films may rely on narration while others let the footage speak for itself.

Interviews are the backbone of most documentary movies. You can easily intercut interviews with other elements, such as archival footage, graphics, pictures, and animation. When the audio portion of interviews is laid over visuals, it is referred to as a voiceover and shouldn't be confused with a narration.

You have infinite choices in what kind of documentary you

KNACK DIGITAL MOVIEMAKING

Documentary Filmmaker

- Digital video has made it much easier for the average person to pick up a camcorder and make a documentary.

- Technically, anything that is "documenting reality" falls into the documentary category. For example, when

you pick up your camcorder and film your cat, you are making a documentary.

- Any good documentary must have a reason for being made. What do you want your audience to take away from the viewing of your film?

Sports Documentaries

- Sports naturally lend themselves to documentary filmmaking. They are filled with interesting characters, action, and conflict.

- The 1994 documentary, *Hoop Dreams,* follows two inner city kids as they try to make their dreams of playing in the NBA come true.

Intended originally to be a thirty-minute short, filming lasted five years resulting in over 250 hours of footage.

- *Murderball,* a documentary about paraplegic athletes who play wheelchair rugby, was shot on an inexpensive digital video camera and nominated for an Oscar.

can make. Many of today's documentaries focus on political and controversial issues. Others may cover sporting events, people, concerts and music, history, travel destinations, or other topics.

If you want your documentary to be full of factual information, you should do an in-depth study of everything to be included in the film. Gather information by searching the Internet, reading books on the subject, and watching other related nonfiction films and TV programs.

Unless you make a propaganda film, try your best not to be biased when presenting information in your documentary. Some would argue, however, that it is impossible to be truly neutral when making a documentary film. The filmmaker's choices and edits can present a biased view. If three different filmmakers were asked to make a documentary on the same story, each story would come out differently.

Good documentaries are always entertaining, informative, and factual.

Rising in Popularity

- Though still not as popular as narrative films, documentaries are becoming more and more popular with audiences.

- Audiences turn to documentaries to find more credible information than what they can get from the mainstream media outlets.

- Amateur filmmakers tend to make documentaries because they are often easier and more affordable to produce than narrative movies.

Cinéma Vérité and Direct Cinema

- Cinéma vérité is a style of documentary started by the French in the 1960s that strives for candid realism by showing people in everyday situations with authentic dialogue.

- Direct cinema is the American version of cinéma vérité. While similar in many ways, the two differ in that cinéma vérité filmmakers use the camera to provoke subjects and reveal stories while direct cinema is strictly observational.

- Direct cinema was made possible by the advent of light, portable cameras and sound recorders.

SHORT FILMS & MUSIC VIDEOS

Many directors working in Hollywood today got their start with shorts and music videos

Short films, short subject films, or simply "shorts" are motion pictures whose lengths are less than forty minutes. Short films were popular from the early 1900s to the 1930s. They were often screened at theaters after feature films. Shorts have become popular again in recent years.

Making short films is often the first step on an aspiring director's road to Hollywood. These films are cheaper and easier to make than feature films; they usually don't take very long to produce; and their length makes shorts more likely to be watched by financial backers and others who want to judge a filmmaker's ability. Shorts offer a way to learn skills, build experience, and showcase talent. The short film format

Film Festivals

- South by Southwest is a music and film festival that takes place every year in Austin, Texas. The festival showcases hundreds of short and feature-length films.

- There are thousands of festivals that take place around the world every year, with many catering exclusively to short films.

- Often these film festivals only cater to certain types of films or filmmakers. For example: Dances with Wolves Festival doesn't allow celebrities.

The Oscars

- The best shorts can go on to win awards and become a calling card for the filmmaker. The Oscars give awards to the best live action and animated short every year.

- A good short could go on to win small cash awards and non-monetary awards at festivals around the country.

- The best short films revolve around a simple story. There simply isn't enough time to properly develop a long list of characters and subplots.

also allows for increased experimentation since most shorts will not be seen by a wide audience.

Digital technology has made creating shorts easier than ever and is providing new ways to bring short content to an audience. Such films can be easily distributed via the Internet where viewers are most likely to watch short films. If you're interested in making movies, a short film might be a great way to get your start.

Unlike most other types of film, music videos have absolutely no limit on content. Some videos tell stories and others illustrate the song's lyrics, while some are just visual poetry inspired by the music. Just like shorts, many filmmakers have made their start directing low budget music videos. They are inexpensive to make and allow a filmmaker to hone his skills.

It shouldn't be that hard to find musicians and bands who want to be in a music video. Find an emerging local band that will let you film its first music video. The budget will be low, and the music may be bad, but the experience will be invaluable.

Music Videos

- The ultimate goal of a music video is to promote the music to help the band sell albums, make fans, and book shows.

- One advantage is that you don't need quality sound equipment, or any sound equipment for that matter, because you will add the music track in post-production.

- David Fincher (*Fight Club, The Curious Case of Benjamin Button*), Michael Bay (*The Rock, Transformers*), and Brett Ratner (*Rush Hour*) are among the filmmakers who got their start directing music videos.

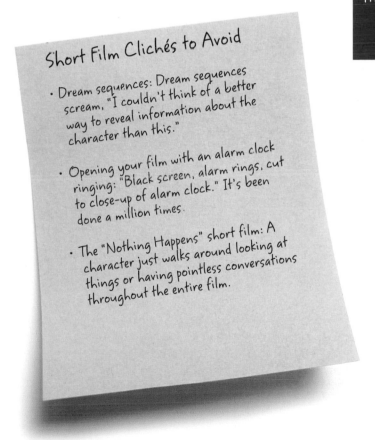

Short Film Clichés to Avoid

- Dream sequences: Dream sequences scream, "I couldn't think of a better way to reveal information about the character than this."

- Opening your film with an alarm clock ringing: "Black screen, alarm rings, cut to close-up of alarm clock." It's been done a million times.

- The "Nothing Happens" short film: A character just walks around looking at things or having pointless conversations throughout the entire film.

COMMERCIALS & SPONSORED FILM
These types of videos are made to convey a special message

Companies spend millions of dollars every year producing television commercials designed to sell a product or promote an idea. Super Bowl–style, big-budgeted commercials are not the only commercials that succeed in doing this. Low budget commercials can make the same impression on a viewer; the key is to make sure that the viewers receive the message.

Watching commercials can teach you a lot about the craft of video production. You can learn even more by shooting a few. You must have a basic understanding of the product you are trying to sell and of the audience that it is targeted to.

Due to their extremely short length, commercials are easy to shoot and edit. However, this limited time also presents its own set of challenges. While they still allow for a certain

Commercials

- Over the years, television advertisements have been used to sell every product imaginable, from goods and services to political campaigns.

- Since TV commercials are the most effective mass-market advertising format, and successful commercials can air

repeatedly for years, companies often spare no expense when producing their short thirty-second spots.

- Most ads are extraordinarily well made, showcasing the latest special effects technologies, great music, popular personalities, and overall great production values.

Sponsored Film

- A sponsored film or industrial film is a type of video that is made by a corporation or organization for internal distribution and use.

- Sponsored film topics can include how-to videos, educational videos, public service shorts, safety

videos, and specialized training videos.

- Sponsored films are not meant to be creative and are only seen by a small audience; however, they don't take a long time to make and the pay is often very good.

amount of creativity, commercials above all must convey their message quickly, clearly, and persuasively.

A great way to get the hang of commercial shooting is to make your own for fun. Pick out a product you like and give it your best shot. If you know someone who owns a store, business, or product, that works even better. This can be a successful way to build up a reel that you can use to get paying gigs in the future.

Commercials for television aren't the only gig in town. While TV commercials aren't going anywhere, online video advertising is in its infancy and growing every day. Producing online ads can be a great way to get your start in the world of profitable video making. Be on the lookout for contests online where companies ask amateur filmmakers to make commercials for them. If your spot is good enough, it could go on to air on television and win you cash and prizes.

How-to

- The Internet is filled with homemade how-to videos that can teach you anything from how to do your taxes to how to cook an enchilada.

- Chances are you have a special knowledge or skill that you could turn into an instructional video for a larger audience's benefit.

- Some Web sites, such as howcast.com and ehow .com, will pay you a flat fee or a percentage of the profits to make how-to videos for them.

Infomercials

- An infomercial is basically a long commercial, typically twenty-eight minutes in length. They often include a spokesperson and a studio audience.

- If you have a product that you want to sell or know somebody who does, make an infomercial to generate sales.

- Making a cheap infomercial isn't difficult. With minimal equipment and the space to film, you can make your own infomercials in just a few hours.

HOME MOVIES & VIRAL VIDEOS

Shoot better-looking home movies and family vacation videos with these practical tips and ideas

When making home movies, the average person tends to pick up the camcorder, point it carelessly, and press the record button. While this can occasionally capture a great moment, most of the time it will result in video that won't be worth watching. Putting in a little extra effort when recording your home movies can result in videos that are of better quality and will be enjoyed for generations.

The best thing you can do to increase the quality of your home movies is to have a plan for them before you start shooting. Have an idea of what the movie is going to be about, what you want to videotape, and what you want the final product to look like. Think about what shots you can get

Online Videos

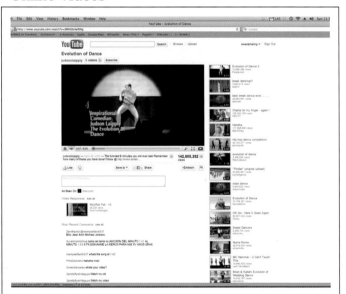

- Online video sharing sites like YouTube have made it possible for you to share your video with a vast audience from all over the world.

- YouTube has a great insight feature which tells you how many views your videos

- receive, how your videos were found, and who watches them.

- If your videos become popular enough, you can apply to be a YouTube partner and earn a share of some of the money that your video generates.

Viral Videos

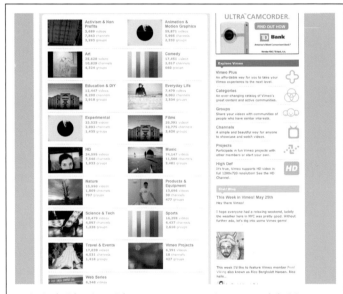

- A viral video is a video that spreads quickly via the Internet. Viral videos are usually short clips on a video-sharing site that people link to in blogs, e-mails, and instant messages.

- It is not uncommon for these types of videos to cre-

- ate Internet celebrities out of their creators.

- Viral video marketing is when a company attempts to create a viral video in order to drive traffic to their Web sites and sell their products or services.

that will make the final video more entertaining and fun to watch.

Unfortunately, most home movies have too much shaky footage, which will make it unwatchable and may even make viewers physically sick. Take your time whenever you are performing a camera move. Don't just whip the camera from place to place at whatever catches your eyes. Avoid using the zoom lens while recording, but if you must, make the zooms quick. Hold your shots for at least seven seconds each. It will seem too long when filming, but having just a few extra seconds of a shot will really make a difference later on when editing.

Try to avoid overshooting. If you're not planning on editing, your video risks being boring. If you plan on editing, having a ton of footage to go through will make the process a lot more time consuming and tedious.

Vacation Videos

- The average person's camcorder will likely see the most use while traveling on vacation.

- The most interesting travel videos focus less on landmarks and more on people; film the locals, film yourself, and film your traveling companion(s).

- Try to resist the urge to narrate while behind the camera. Instead, step in front of the camera and talk into it.

- Shoot a lot of close-ups. Get in close with your camera to add detail, variety, and style to your vacation video.

Tips for Going Viral

- Post your video on every video-sharing site that you can find. Promote your viral video by sending the link to everyone you know and post your video on forums and social networking sites.

- Keep the video short, preferably less than a minute. The shorter the video, the more likely people will watch your video repeatedly.

- Make your video funny. Most videos that go viral are comedies.

- Worry less about quality and more about content. It actually may be preferable to have a video that looks amateurish because it makes the video seem more real.

- Keep trying. You can't predict what video will go viral so you may have to make quite a few until one eventually does.

WRITING A SCREENPLAY
Writing a script takes hard work and a dedication to your story

Screenplays have been a key element of filmmaking since the earliest days of Hollywood. Writing a movie script may seem simple at first, but there are many components to writing a good screenplay. As a screenwriter, you must be able to express visual ideas through writing, creating both engaging characters and a tight story structure.

The saying "show, don't tell" is especially true of screen-writing. Great scripts are chock full of visuals that move the story along and provide movement for your readers.

Even though you might want to write what your characters think, you must discipline yourself not to. Internal monologues have no place in scripts. Rather, external behavior can be expressed through dialogue or physical actions. The camera can go anywhere your imagination wants it to go, and

KNACK DIGITAL MOVIEMAKING

Stage versus Screen

- The main difference between writing for film versus writing for stage is in the amount of dialogue used.

- Plays are mainly about the actor's words, while films have fewer spoken words and many more images.

- Writers for stage and screen have the same goal, to tell a good story, but the story is told in different ways.

Competition

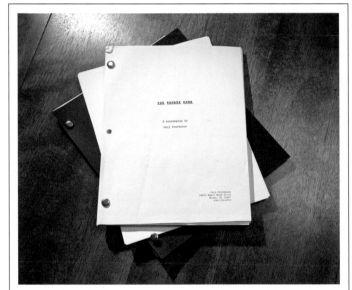

- Every year thousands of people try to write the Greatest Screenplay of All Time.

- Getting your script noticed by über-busy Hollywood executives can sometimes be harder than actually writing the screenplay.

- The best way to get your screenplay read by producers is to hire an agent who can help get it into the right hands.

- Many studios won't read screenplays not submitted to them by an agent.

audiences expect to be visually entertained.

Writing good screenplays is a skill that can be learned. Good writing takes practice and perseverance. Your first screenplay may not get you any awards, but keep writing. The more scripts you write, the better you will become.

Writing a Documentary

- Because narrative films are fiction and documentaries are based on fact, doing extensive and accurate research takes the place of writing a fictionalized story.

- When making a documentary, the script is often written after you complete filming so you know what you have shot.

- A shooting script should be written for a documentary if the event you will capture can be predicted.

Perseverance

- To become better at something, you must practice it every day. Writing is no different.

- Set apart a certain time of the day to write and stick to it. Many people start writing a screenplay but never end up finishing it because they get distracted by other things.

- Make working on your screenplay part of your daily routine; you will be more likely to see it through to the end.

FINDING INSPIRATION

Here are some exercises to try that may help you come up with story ideas

If you want to write a script, then you are going to need a story. A successful scriptwriter must actively seek out story ideas. Staring at a blank page for hours on end and expecting an exciting and original story idea to pop into your head is not going to generate results.

Great writers train themselves to notice and store their ideas

so they always have a lot to work with when it comes down to writing. These writers don't often struggle to find inspiration and ideas; instead they have a hard time writing them all into something an audience would want to see.

Get into the habit of recording every idea or interesting fact that you come across throughout your day. The quicker you

Finding Stories

- Newspaper and magazine articles are great places to find real life story ideas. Sometimes fact is indeed stranger than fiction.

- Reading human interest articles can give you the basis of a story from which you can build.

- Look for articles that leave you wondering more about what, how, and, most importantly, why certain events happened the way they did.

- Reading published fiction can also inspire you with new thoughts, characters, ideas, and themes.

Family Stories

- You may be surprised how many interesting and original stories that your friends and family have.

- Stories that have been passed down by your family from generation to generation are often completely original and filled with

intriguing characters, and can be turned into an excellent screenplay.

- Some writers carry around a notebook so they can quickly jot down story ideas and bits of dialogue as they hear them.

can write it down the better. Don't tell yourself, "That's a great idea. I'll remember that later." You won't. You will likely forget important details or forget it altogether.

A great story will not come to you fully formed. You have to work to find ideas that you can build a coherent story from. The source of every piece of inspiration is that small idea. Start out by noticing your ideas and putting them down on paper.

STORY

Exercise

- Exercising gets the blood flowing, releases endorphins, and can be a very effective way to find inspiration for your story.

- Get up, get outside, and work up a sweat. Going for a long run will clear your head and give you time to think over story ideas.

- You will be amazed what you come up with after a twenty-minute run.

- Exercising has the added benefit of keeping you in shape.

Free Writing

- Free writing is an exercise where you write as fast, freely, and carelessly as possible for a set amount of time.

- Do not stop to correct spelling or grammar. Let your thoughts wander off topic without care.

- Free writing will lead to large chunks of unusable material but can also lead to thoughts and ideas that you would not normally come up with.

- Once you finish, read what you wrote out loud and see what you came up with.

STORY, CONFLICT, CHARACTER
The essential elements that will make your screenplay great

Conflict, character, and structure are the three main elements in your screenplay that will make your screenplay exciting. You must create a goal for your protagonist, devise a main obstacle that is preventing him from achieving that goal, and break this obstacle down into smaller obstacles. Ask yourself, what is the protagonist's goal? What is he trying to achieve and what is preventing him from achieving it?

Many different types of conflict can be in a single screenplay, and can involve most, if not all of the characters. Conflict drives the story and the characters. Ideally, the audience will relate to your protagonist and the conflicts he or she faces.

Each scene has its own structure with a beginning, middle, and end and should contribute to the overall structure of the story. Every scene should include the following elements:

Premise

- The movie's premise—or foundation—is a central idea, an intriguing setup, or a situation that will drive the plot and make people want to watch your movie.

- You should be able to boil down your premise to a very short sentence, around twenty-five to thirty words max.

- The premise is sometimes typed out on the cover page of your script and other times it is simply used as a motivational tool for the writer, ensuring that he sticks to his story.

Types of Conflict

- There are several different overarching themes of conflict in movies:

- Man versus Self: A type of conflict where the character must deal with an internal problem or struggle.

- Man versus Man: When the character's main conflict comes from the actions of another character.

- Man versus Society: The character may face conflict with the values of society or society at large.

- Man versus Nature: When a character battles against the forces of nature.

setting, character, action, and dialogue. Each character in a scene should have an objective or need, and the tension created by these needs should build throughout the scene.

Create interesting characters and develop them as the foundation of your story. The audience should see different sides of the characters, understand how they think and act, and learn about their attitudes and ideas about life. The story should influence the character and the character should influence the story.

Great characters are three-dimensional. They should be both believable and interesting. Before writing a character you should create his backstory. Decide on his background, appearance, occupation, and unique traits. Know how he talks, his mannerisms, facial expressions, and body language. Develop your character's interests, habits, and ambitions. This practice will create realistic characters that will come alive to the audience.

Characters

- Good characters for screenplays and all forms of fiction are often drawn from people you know in real life.

- Take note of the fun, interesting, quirky, and unique qualities of the people around you. Use them to make dynamic characters for your story.

- However, you must be careful not to go overboard. Above all, your characters must seem real and relatable.

Writing Dialogue

- Dialogue in movies is not the same as dialogue in real life. Real life dialogue is full of repetition, interruptions, and irrelevances.

- Dialogue in film must have purpose. It must move the story forward, reveal character, or give important information.

- Dialogue should be kept as short as possible. Less is more. Characters shouldn't state the obvious or talk about how they feel.

- Great dialogue is filled with subtext. Subtext reveals the motives and thoughts of your character without actually saying it.

THREE-ACT STRUCTURE

Most movies are based on a simple story structure that dates back thousands of years

The three-act structure is a type of dramatic story structure that originated in the golden age of Greek theater, around 500–300 B.C. Aristotle's Poetics stated that stories should be divided into three acts, with a beginning, middle, and end.

Act I is the setup. It introduces the characters, their relationships to each other, and the world in which they live. Halfway through the first act, the inciting incident, catalyst, or call to action occurs, which throws the protagonist's everyday life out of balance. This leads to the end of Act I, or Plot Point 1. Plot Point 1 is the first big turning point in your script, the point that pushes the character into Act II.

Act II is the longest of the acts and is often the hardest to

The Hook

- Within the first ten pages of your screenplay, or five to ten minutes of your movie, you must have a hook that grabs the audience's attention and draws them into the story.

- Here you need to introduce the main characters, establish the genre, and let the reader or viewer know generally what the story is about, and what is at stake.

- The hook should raise a question in the viewer's mind.

- A good hook needs to show character and create conflict.

Three-act Structure

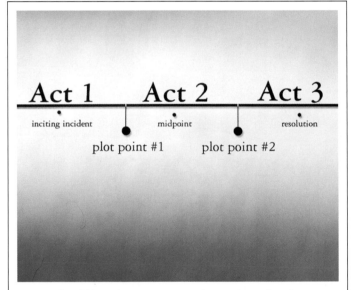

- Act I should last about twenty-five to thirty-five pages or a quarter of the movie's length and include the hook, an inciting incident, and end with Plot Point 1.

- Act II is the longest act and runs roughly 50 percent of the total running time or sixty to eighty pages and ends with Plot Point 2.

- Act III can be anywhere from twenty to thirty pages to just a few pages long. It includes the climax and resolution.

write. As the act progresses, the problem facing the character established in Plot Point 1 should continue to escalate, eventually leading to a point in the story where your protagonist's strength, willpower, and faith hit rock bottom. Near the end of the act, the protagonist gets a ray of hope (Plot Point 2) that leads him toward the climax. Act III of the story resolves the main problem and answers questions about any subplots, leaving the audience with a satisfying ending.

There have been successful movies that do not strictly follow a three-act structure. This type of story structure should be looked at as a guideline, rather than a set of rules that you must follow. However, audiences have been trained to recognize that this is how a story should be told and breaking the audience's expectations could result in an unwatchable movie.

Star Wars

- *Star Wars* is a good example of a movie with a three-act structure. The inciting incident in Act I is when Princess Leia is captured and sends off her droids with important information.

- Plot Point 1 occurs when Luke finds his aunt and uncle murdered, and he commits to helping Obi-Wan Kenobi fight the empire.

- Act II takes up the middle part of the movie and ends with Luke's escaping from the Death Star.

- In Act III, Luke blows up the Death Star and saves the Rebellion.

The Four-act Structure

- The four-act structure is basically a three-act structure with the second act broken into two parts, making it easier to write a long second act.

- The first act remains unchanged and the third act becomes the fourth act.

- The new second act will have the hero beginning his journey, facing conflict and obstacles that lead to a turning point at the end of the act. This turning point must change the course of the story but keep the hero pursuing the same goal.

- The third act starts with a ray of hope but then quickly starts the conflicts over again, leading to a low point that feeds the climax and resolution in Act IV.

WRITING AN OUTLINE

Write an outline of your story before you dive into writing your full script

Writing an outline before you tackle writing the script has many benefits. Having an outline by your side helps you create a strong structure that keeps you on course while writing the first draft of your script.

Poor organization is one of the main reasons screenplays fail. Many beginning writers avoid this step, thinking that the story will reveal itself as they write. This often leads to a script that is not cohesive. Knowing where your story is going and how it will end will prevent you from leading the audience along pointless tangents that don't pull the story forward. An outline will help you visualize how the main story and any subplot will play out before you write.

Log Line

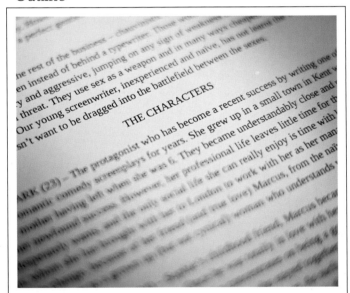

- A log line is a simple, very concise, one-sentence explanation of a movie's main story.

- When reviewing a screenplay, the first thing any potential buyer will want to see is the script's log line.

- You should write your log line before you start writing your screenplay to help keep you focused on the story you wish to tell.

- A successful log line explains the main concept of your story in one concise sentence (twenty-five words or less).

Outline

- An outline is a one- or two-page summary of your screenplay that can help ensure your screenplay is cohesive and logical.

- Write down the concept, characters, and outcome of the story, or make a list of major bullet points for scenes with little to no dialogue.

- Since an outline is personalized to help you, the screenwriter, you do not need to follow a specific format.

Keeping an outline brief still allows you to make changes to the story before and during the writing of your script. The outline does not have to be followed strictly; it is just a tool to help loosely guide you. While writing your script, it is very likely you will develop new ideas, characters, and subplots.

Start by making a bulleted list that describes what happens in the major scenes. You don't have to go into great detail. Avoid anything that is not important to the central idea of the scene, such as dialogue and minor characters. Each bullet point should only be one to two sentences long.

Next, expand this list to include the scenes that carry you from one major scene to another.

Once you finish, go back and reread your outline, and cut any scenes that do not move the story forward. It is much easier to make changes now to your outline than later on when you have a full script written.

Treatment

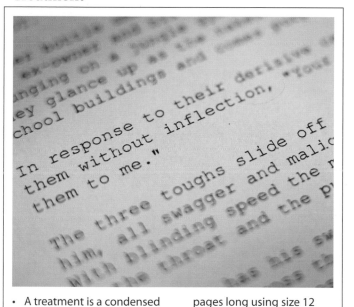

- A treatment is a condensed version of a screenplay, written in the format of a short story in paragraph form.

- A treatment can help get your story straight and fine-tune the details.

- It should be single spaced, and about seven to fifteen pages long using size 12 Times New Roman or Courier font.

- Each scene should be described in two to four sentences.

- Avoid giving camera directions, but include some dialogue snippets.

The Scriptment

- A scriptment is a cross between a full script and a treatment and includes significantly more dialogue than a treatment.

- Scriptments vary in complexity; some may describe the film shot to shot rather than scene to scene and have lengthy dialogue that is formatted exactly as it is in a finished script.

- Writing a scriptment may not always be necessary, but an agent or producer will sometimes request one.

- The term was coined by James Cameron, who often writes detailed scriptments while developing his movies.

SCREENPLAY FORMAT & SOFTWARE

Screenplays must be formatted in a very specific way; software can do that for you

Screenplays must be written in a specific format that Hollywood has used for decades. Producers and agents will not look at a script if it does not adhere to industry standards, which include specifics on format and language. You must stick to conventions covering everything from the number of pages to the type of font used. Depart from the accepted format,

and you risk having your script prejudged as amateurish.

You should write in the present tense because you want the movie to play in the reader's head as they read the screenplay. Use an active voice, such as, "Tyler throws a baseball." Do not use a passive voice, such as, "Tyler threw a baseball."

The first time a character appears in the script, the character's

Cover Sheet

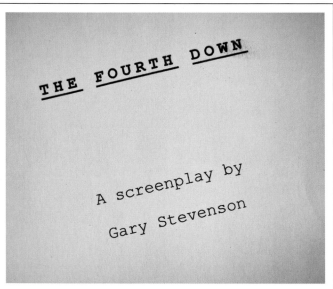

- Every script starts with a cover sheet, or title page.

- The title of your screenplay should be centered, one third of the way down the page. It can be in all uppercase and/or in quotes and/ or underlined.

- The word "by" is centered two lines under the title with the author(s) name following two lines under that.

- Your name, address, phone number, and e-mail address belong in the lower right corner of the page.

Courier Font

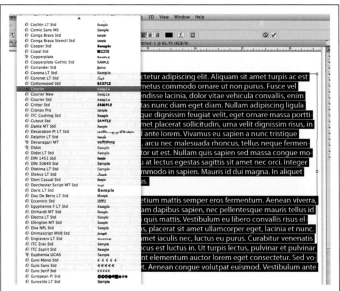

- All scripts must be written in size 12 Courier (not Courier New) font. The only exceptions are the Courier fonts that are used in popular screenwriting programs.

- Courier is a monospaced font, so every character is the same width. Mono-

spaced fonts ensure uniformity because only a certain number of letters will fit on each line and each page.

- This uniformity leads to one page of a screenplay averaging one minute of screen time.

name must be written in all uppercase letters. When a character speaks, his name always appears in all uppercase letters above his lines of dialogue. A character name can be an actual name (JOE), description (OLD MAN), or occupation (PAINTER).

Do not describe camera directions within the script because the directions can disrupt the flow of the story for the reader. Do not use the word CAMERA to describe what the audience is supposed to see. Instead use "we" (i.e., "we follow," instead of "the camera follows").

Scene headings are required anytime your character moves to a new location or setting. Scene headings are written on one line in all uppercase letters with some words abbreviated. For example, a scene that takes place inside a bar at night would have the scene heading "INT. BAR – NIGHT." Interiors are always abbreviated "INT." while exteriors are abbreviated "EXT."

Rather than having to learn the proper Hollywood script format, many screenwriters use software that formats the script as they write, allowing the writer to concentrate on the story rather than the formatting.

Proper Format

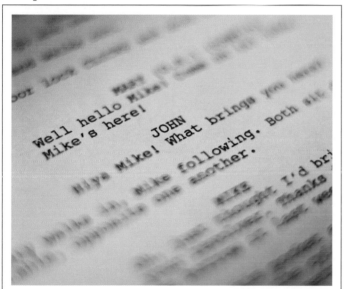

- Screenplays are written on standard 8½- by 11-inch white three-hole punched paper and bound together with Acco No. 5 round-head brass fasteners.

- The top and bottom margins are between .5 and 1 inch, the left margin is between 1.2 and 1.6 inches, and the right margin is between .5 and 1 inch.

- The average screenplay is between ninety-five and 125 pages long, with comedies running on the shorter end and dramas on the longer end.

Software

- The Movie Magic Screenwriter and Final Draft are two of the most popular industry standard screenwriting programs. These programs eliminate some of the formatting hassles and allow you to just write.

- You should download a trial version before you make the decision to buy either of these programs.

- If you would rather not pay for software, free software options, such as CeltX, can be found online.

- Screenwriting templates for Microsoft Word can also be found online.

BREAKING DOWN THE SCRIPT
Doing a script breakdown makes the work you have ahead of you more manageable

Now that you have your script, it's almost time to shoot your movie. Before you can, however, one of the first items on your agenda will be to do a script breakdown. On big budget films with a large crew, this task is usually handled by the first assistant director. On low budget productions, the responsibility will fall on the filmmakers themselves. It is not hard to break

down your script, but doing so will greatly help you plan and schedule your shoot days.

Breaking down a script is the process of logging each significant element needed for production of a scene, such as cast, costumes, special effects, and stunts, and then transferring them onto what's called a breakdown sheet.

Start the Breakdown

- To begin a script breakdown, go through the entire script and draw a line across the page separating each scene.

- A new scene is determined when a change in location or a change in time happens.

- When the number of characters in the scene changes dramatically, a new scene may also begin.

- Assign each scene a number that will stay with that scene throughout your production.

Lining the Script

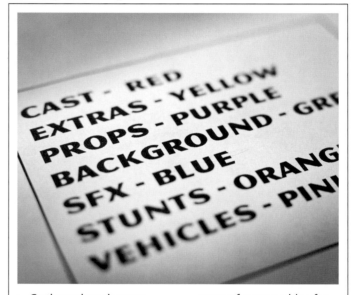

- Go through each scene with a few highlighters or colored pencils and highlight each different element that is needed in a scene. This is called lining the script.

- The Hollywood standard is to use red for any speaking parts, green for extras,

orange for stunts, blue for special effects, purple for props, pink for vehicles/animals, and brown for on set sound effects/music.

- Feel free to use your own colors, but be sure to add a key at the beginning of the script so others can understand.

The main purpose for breaking down the script is to create a means of communication and documentation between the production team and the various departments so that they are informed of the necessary elements of a scene and who is responsible for them. If a piece of equipment, a prop, or a light isn't on location when you need it, you can't shoot that scene. Another reason to break down your script is so you can make an accurate budget, which can't be completed until you've identified all the items that you will need during production.

Breakdown Sheet

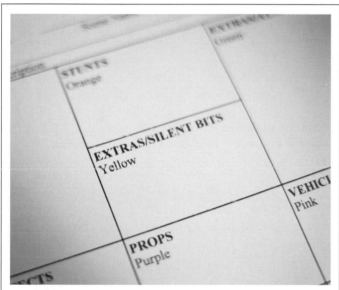

- The next step is to transfer all of the information from your lined script to a script breakdown sheet for each scene.

- The top of the breakdown sheet should have lines for you to write the production name, date, scene number and name, location name, interior/exterior, day/night, and a brief description of the scene.

- The rest of the breakdown sheet is where you will fill in the color-coded information from your lined script.

Production Strip Board

- The production strip board is a cardboard or wooden chart that has color-coded strips of paper tacked on it.

- These strips contain information about the scenes in your script.

- The strips can be easily removed and rearranged based on scheduling changes.

- Each strip on the board will contain the scene number, day/night, interior/exterior, continuity, and the scene length in eighths.

PREPARATION

BUDGETING
Having an organized budget lets you know exactly where your money will be spent

Developing an accurate and thorough budget is an essential pre-production step. Your budget must be low enough to attract investors but high enough to get the job done. You may end up making multiple drafts of your budget in an attempt to reduce costs as you get closer to your film's start date. Even Hollywood executives, whose job it is to predict film costs, rarely can do so accurately. There are many variables and unforeseen costs that will come up during your film's production, making it impossible to plan for every penny spent.

With that said, a film's budget is the first thing any potential investor wants to see, so it is important to be as accurate and

Above the Line

- Above the line costs refer to any costs that are spent before the actual filming of your production begins.

- Screenplay rights and salaries for creative talents such as the screenwriter, director, producer, and actors are all above the line costs.

- Hollywood movies often spend 50 percent of their budget on above the line costs while low budget films may have little or no above the line costs.

Below the Line

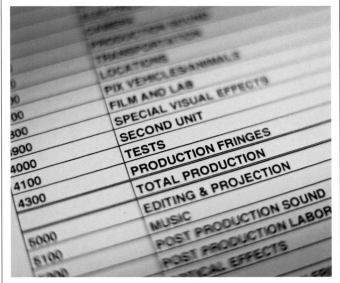

- Below the lines costs refer to the costs of non-starring cast and technical crew, equipment rentals, travel, insurance, legal fees, post-production expenses, etc.

- On a low budget film, most of your costs will likely be below the line.

- The script details, not the length, will determine the total below the line costs.

- Try to plan for every expense that you may run into over the course of production.

realistic as possible. It may initially seem like a good idea to strive for a low budget to attract investors, but this method can lead to much suffering later on. If you don't have enough money to cover production costs, the film will likely come in over budget. Worse, you will end up with a subpar film. Trying to stick to an unrealistic budget will force you to constantly compromise, leading to a low-quality finished film.

If you already own a camera, lights, sound equipment, and have your locations secured, your operational costs may be quite low. Be aware of the costs associated with every phase of production. Many beginning filmmakers spend too much money during filming and have nothing left for post-production. Do not overlook items such as props, tools, gasoline for generators and cars, rentals, permits, and catering. If you are able to convince your cast and crew to work for free, do not skimp on good food. Ultimately, the research and preparation you do now will play a big part in determining if you still have money in your pocket when the credits roll.

Typical Hollywood Budget

- Buying story rights can cost anywhere from a few grand to upward of $10 million.

- Directors typically earn 7 percent of the film's total budget with A-list directors commanding $5 to $10 million a film.

- A-list actors can make $20-$30 million a film plus perks and a percentage of the gross profits. Conversely, extras earn $50-$100 a day.

- Depending on the film, visual effects can cost upward of $100 million.

- A film's music budget averages around 8 percent of its final total.

Budget Template

- If you need help creating a budget, there are a lot of software options available.

- Movie Magic Budgeting and Gorilla Film Production are popular but expensive software choices.

- You most likely won't need to use expensive film bud-geting software unless you are creating a very detailed and high budget film.

- If you don't have software, you can use a Microsoft Excel spreadsheet to create a budget. Free Excel templates for film budgeting can be found online, or you can make your own.

SCOUTING LOCATIONS

Check out different places to see if they would be suitable sets for your film

Location scouting is a vital process in the pre-production stage of filmmaking. Scriptwriters, producers, or directors decide what kind of scenery they would like to use for the parts of the film that are shot off set. A search for a suitable place or "location" is then started. You should look for interesting locations that will add to the film's story.

Be sure to scout at several times because locations can change depending on the hour. It's wise to check your spot on the day of the week and the time of day that you'll be filming. A park may be empty at 1:00 p.m. on a Tuesday but busy during that time on a Friday.

Many locations require that you have permits and legal

Scouting

- When scouting locations for filming, the most important thing is to find a place that matches the setting of your story.

- Keep in mind that many locations require that you have a permit and permis-

sion to shoot there. You will need to know in advance if you will be allowed to film at a certain place.

- Make sure there is enough room to set up and take into consideration the ease of access and parking.

Record Your Location

- While scouting, bring a still camera and take wide panoramic photos of the location for future reference.

- Bring a video camera with headphones to monitor the sound and take sample video at different angles.

- Another thing to consider is whether or not the location has adequate cell phone service.

- In addition, take written notes to refer back to at a later time.

permission to shoot. Many states require you have $1 million of general liability insurance before they will allow shooting on state property. See the resources section for more on permits and legal permissions.

Cemeteries, malls, grocery stores, corporations, and businesses are all private properties and require you get permission. Most private business owners will be happy to let you use their property for filming if you ask politely. Make sure you won't block traffic or disturb neighbors, as this will surely draw the attention of the police.

Check the Light

- Check the ambient light of a location at different times of the day in overcast sky and bright sun so you know how lighting will affect your shoot in advance.

- A camcorder will help determine how the light looks on video.

- For indoor locations, see how natural light reacts with blinds, doors, and windows open and closed.

Power Outlets

- Check the availability of power sources on location to see if there is a suitable place to connect your lights or any other equipment you may need that requires power.

- If there is an outlet you can use, determine how long of an extension cord you will need to reach it.

- Check to see if you can get to the fuse (breaker) box in case you lose power.

PREPARATION

41

SCHEDULING

Put together an accurate schedule before you shoot to save yourself time and money

When making a schedule you are trying to figure out two main things: how many days you need to film, and what scenes will be shot when and in what order.

Use your breakdown sheet to determine how many days it will take to shoot your film. Try to find scenes that can be shot together on the same day to tighten the schedule. Keep your

budget in mind: You will have to make your budget fit your schedule. If you only have a few hundred dollars, you will not be able to film your movie over a three-month period.

Try to film all the scenes at one location consecutively; jumping back and forth between multiple scene locations will cost you time and money. Scheduling that takes place

Note Cards

- A good way to get started with determining your film's schedule is to write down every scene on a note card, spread each card out on a table, and start putting them together like a puzzle.

- This will help you visualize the flow of the shooting

schedule and make it easy to rearrange the order in which you shoot.

- Try to shoot in sequence as much as possible to help your actors stay in character and to maximize the use of your location.

Bad Weather

- Schedule outdoor scenes early on in your production so that you can reschedule them later if the forecast calls for bad weather.

- When you shoot outside, have a backup plan, such as another indoor location

that you can go to if it starts to rain during filming.

- Monitor the weather days before any outdoor shoot to make sure you get the weather the script calls for.

during production will be tricky. You will have to film certain scenes during the day, scenes at night, scenes in certain weather conditions, and film within specific establishments. Schedule accordingly to keep your production moving smoothly.

You need to know which actors are needed for which scenes, and then schedule the scenes so that you maximize the actor's talent but minimize the number of days he is used. Ideally, your cast and crew will always be available to shoot, but this is not realistic. Keeping track of everyone requires a lot of follow up phone calls and e-mails. If one person can't make it to a shoot, then you will need to reorganize the whole day . . . again.

Shooting Schedule

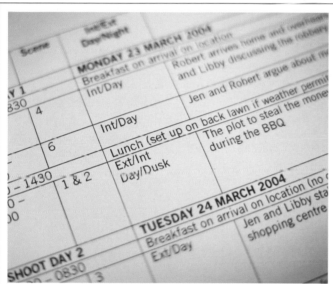

- Once you have a general idea of the order of the locations, it is time to put together a best case scenario shooting schedule.

- Shooting schedules can be made using dedicated software, such as CeltX, or they can be made using a Microsoft Excel spreadsheet.

- Take into consideration all of your cast and crew's availability, and try your best to schedule around any days when they will not be available.

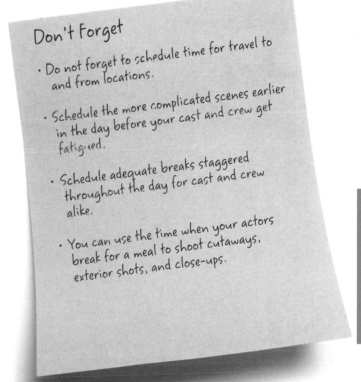

Don't Forget

- Do not forget to schedule time for travel to and from locations.

- Schedule the more complicated scenes earlier in the day before your cast and crew get fatigued.

- Schedule adequate breaks staggered throughout the day for cast and crew alike.

- You can use the time when your actors break for a meal to shoot cutaways, exterior shots, and close-ups.

STORYBOARDS & SHOTLIST

Even if you can't draw, making storyboards is an important step in pre-visualizing your film

Making storyboards allows you to test complicated setups cheaply on paper instead of expensively on location.

When drawing and visualizing your film, you'll find places in the script where your story doesn't work. There may be gaps or jumps in your story that you didn't notice before. It is much better to notice mistakes now when you can still fix them than having to deal with them on set, or worse, while editing. Additionally, you may come up with new visual ideas that change the way you imagined the scenes when you originally wrote them. Having storyboards will help you on set when you are having trouble remembering how you wanted to shoot a scene.

Drawing Your Storyboard

- You can make your storyboard frames as large as an entire piece of 8½ x 11 paper or you can shrink them down to fit four to six frames on one piece of paper.

- Use arrows and boxes to show character and camera movement within a scene.

- Leave space underneath the frames to write down any details of the shot, such as scene number, camera moves, etc.

Displaying Your Storyboards

- Once your storyboards are complete, you can hang them on a board or wall in the shooting order or the order in which they will play out in the finished movie.

- It is easy to rearrange them on the board to visualize how different shots will flow together.

- Alternatively, you can scan the images into your computer and animate them to get an even better idea of how your finished movie will look.

Storyboarding can be time consuming and tedious, but it can also be fun. Start your storyboarding by drawing out an easy scene somewhere in the middle of the script. It may not be necessary to storyboard every scene in your film, but you should take the time to draw out the more complicated sequences. You do not need to draw well or spend a lot of time on each storyboard. What is important is that the visuals easily communicate your vision of what the shot should look like.

ZOOM

Some directors simply scratch a quick sketch of a scene on a napkin before they shoot while others rely heavily on creating detailed storyboards. Alfred Hitchcock took storyboarding so seriously that he considered it to be the phase of production where the movie was actually created.

Shotlist

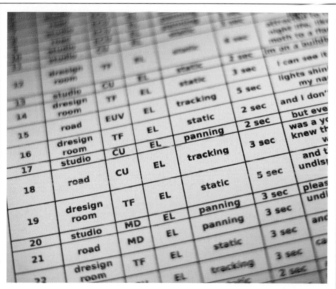

- A shotlist is a list that has every shot that you need for the entire movie, separated by scene. It often goes hand-in-hand with the storyboard.

- The list is often based on your storyboards, or, simply, your storyboards without the drawings.

- The shotlist contains little more than the shot number, shot description, the action that takes place, and the scene number.

- Using a shotlist while filming will ensure that you get all the coverage and shots that you need.

Storyboarding Software

- If stick figure drawings aren't cutting it, or drawing out every shot is too time consuming and tedious, there are many software programs available that can help you in the storyboarding process.

- These programs come with stock libraries filled with actors, props, and other figures that you place in a frame to create your shot.

- Advanced storyboarding software packages allow you to use camera movement and 3D figures to create professional-quality storyboards.

FUNDRAISING

Films require money; be persistent and creative in getting it

Once you have a solid story idea, the script is written, and you've worked out your schedule and budget, it is time to figure out how you are going to get the money to create your masterpiece.

Making a quality film is not cheap. You have to buy or rent a camcorder, sound equipment, lights, and tape stock. You may need to buy or rent an editing system. Throughout the course of production, you will find countless ways to spend money.

Your film can get funded multiple ways, the most common being through investors, prepaying on credit cards, grants, and favors. The most successful fundraisers are filmmakers who know their projects and have the ability to develop personal relationships with the financing person or organization.

Investors

- Be enthusiastic about your project when you approach an investor about financing your film.

- Be honest with any potential investors. Financing a film is a risky endeavor, and the investor may not get his money back, let alone make a profit.

- Look for investors who are more excited about the process of making a movie than making a large profit.

Credit Cards

- Using a credit card or multiple credit cards to fund your film should only be done as a last resort when all other financing options have been exhausted.

- The advantage with credit card financing is that you get your money instantly and it is easy to track where your money is spent.

- Credit cards usually have high interest rates and whatever you borrow you have to pay back, so invest wisely.

When going after funding, have in hand a well-written, solid proposal to convince a prospective buyer that he must invest in your project. The proposal's introduction must hook the investor and draw him into reading the rest of your proposal.

The document should describe exactly what your film is: the title, the log line, what's it about, the genre, the characters, where it's set, the conflict, what happens, and how it might end. Describe why audiences will want to see your film and why you are the only person who has the ability to make it. All of this must be done in four to eight dynamite pages.

Friends & Family

- If your budget is low, you may be able to get a large portion of it funded simply by donations or loans from friends and family.

- Set up an online blog or Web site where people can submit donations. You may be surprised by how many people are willing to donate.

- Money has a way of ruining personal relationships, so be careful when borrowing from friends and family.

Grants

- Many filmmakers have had success getting grants from government programs and charities.

- Applying for grants takes a lot of time, research, and paperwork.

- You will have better luck when applying for grants from charities if your film helps support their cause.

- Many filmmakers try to go this route, so having a strong idea and a well-written proposal will be key to separate yourself from the pack.

CHOOSING THE RIGHT CAMERA

There are a myriad of camera choices; narrow them down and buy based on your need

The digital camcorders of today are smaller and more capable than ever. They come in a variety of shapes, sizes, and colors. You can buy a camcorder that fits almost any budget, from basic entry level to high-end professional models.

Buying a camcorder is a lot like buying a car. A sports car may be the best fit for one person while a minivan is the best fit for another. Will you be filming action sports or interviewing people? Do you want a camera that is small enough to carry with you everywhere? There is no one "right" camera; instead, choose one that best fits your needs.

Most camcorders come with both a viewfinder and an LCD screen. The size and performance in sunlight of the LCD

Comfort

- Check to see if the camcorder fits comfortably in your hand. Are you able to reach the important buttons with your hand in the strap?

- Check the size and weight. Carry it around the store. Is

this a camcorder that you would be comfortable carrying around with you?

- Go through the camcorder's menu features. Is the menu easy to navigate? Do you prefer touch screen menus or another version?

CCD and CMOS

- Most camcorders use either a CCD (charge coupled device) image sensor or a CMOS (complementary metal oxide semiconductor) sensor. Both transform the light captured by camcorders into a digital signal.

- The physical size of the sensor matters: Larger sensors

capture more light.

- Both CCD and CMOS imagers can offer excellent imaging performance.

- CCDs produce better-looking images. However, newer CMOS sensors have improved in some applications.

screen will vary from camcorder to camcorder.

Image stabilization is a feature found in camcorders to reduce jittery video caused by shaky hands. There are two kinds of image stabilization: optical and digital. Optical image stabilization is the better and costlier system. Different manufacturers have different names for this feature, such as Vibration Reduction (VR), Super Steady Shot (SSS), and MegaOIS, among others.

Be sure to consider a camera's battery life, as running out of batteries while shooting can be very annoying, wasting both time and money. Most camcorders come with batteries that give you at least an hour of recording time.

Look for a camcorder with the microphone at the front of the camera rather than on top. Make sure the camcorder has a port for plugging in an external microphone.

Camcorder manufacturers release new models all of the time, so do research, both online and in stores, to find the model that is the best for you.

Optical Zoom

- A camera with 10x optical zoom will bring you ten times closer to your subject. One with 40x zoom will bring you forty times closer.

- Digital camcorders have both an optical zoom and a digital zoom.

- Digital zoom is not real zoom. It works by enlarging a portion of the image to simulate optical zoom at the expense of image quality. Using digital zoom will make your video look pixilated. Look for a camcorder with a high optical zoom and ignore the digital zoom number.

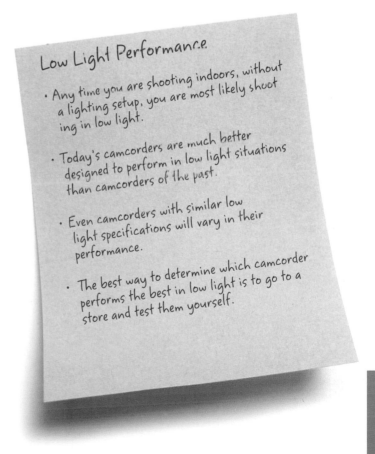

Low Light Performance

- Any time you are shooting indoors, without a lighting setup, you are most likely shooting in low light.

- Today's camcorders are much better designed to perform in low light situations than camcorders of the past.

- Even camcorders with similar low light specifications will vary in their performance.

- The best way to determine which camcorder performs the best in low light is to go to a store and test them yourself.

FORMATS & MEDIA TYPES

A brief overview of the different types of media that camcorders record on

Of all the decisions to make when buying a camcorder, the most important one is picking the media type that your camcorder records to. There are a few different media types that are used. The common medium formats are flash memories, hard drives, MiniDVs, and MiniDVDs.

Flash memory is an increasingly popular storage format for camcorders. Flash memory is solid-state, meaning that it has no moving parts, unlike a hard drive. Due to its lack of moving parts, flash memory is less likely to break or to be damaged, making it the most durable type of camcorder. In addition, there are waterproof, dustproof, and freezeproof options available.

Flash Media

- Flash media camcorders commonly use SD (Secure Digital) cards for recording.

- The amount of footage you can record depends on the size of the SD card you have. Currently, SD card capacities range from 8MB to 32GB. SD cards of the future may hold up to 2TB.

- Nearly every camcorder manufacturer has camcorders in their line that record to SD cards.

- Given the tiny size of flash memory, flash memory camcorders can be very small and light.

Hard Disk Drive

- These camcorders record directly to an onboard hard drive.

- The larger the hard drive, the more hours of footage you can record.

- You will need to transfer your footage to a computer or delete it once your hard drive fills up.

- This same hard disk is used throughout the life of the camcorder so you never need to pay for new tapes or disks.

Hard drive camcorders are also known as hard disk drive camcorders. Hard disk drive camcorders use the abbreviation HDD, which is commonly confused with HD, which is high definition, although HDD camcorders can be HD. An HDD camera allows you to easily find, delete, and rearrange footage without rewinding or fast forwarding. Transferring the recordings to a computer is faster and as uncomplicated as copying computer files. You can also skip across the recorded footage and find particular spots very easily.

Even though the MiniDV format is slowly being replaced by newer formats, it still offers a number of advantages. MiniDV tapes are cheap, widely available, and are great for archiving footage. Footage from a MiniDV generally produces great image quality and is easy to edit. Some manufacturers have stopped making MiniDV cameras completely while others only make the technology available in their high-end models. Many casual videographers, independent filmmakers, and TV production crews still use MiniDVs, so the format will be around for years to come.

MiniDV

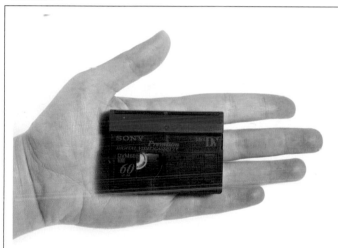

- A MiniDV tape records one hour of footage. Tapes are compact, easy to store, and inexpensive.

- To transfer footage from a MiniDV tape to a computer you must have a FireWire (IEEE 1394) port and cable. MiniDV transfers in real time, so one hour of footage takes one hour to transfer.

- The picture quality of MiniDV camcorders is generally excellent and often better than the other media formats.

MiniDVD

- MiniDVD camcorders record onto 3-inch DVD discs that can be played in most DVD players after you finish shooting.

- MiniDVD camcorders record in a format that is not ideal for editing.

- MiniDVD camcorders were popular a few years ago, but they are being replaced by flash and HDD formats.

- Unless the ability to instantly record your footage to a DVD is a priority, avoid camcorders that record to MiniDVD.

BUYING USED

You can find great deals on used cameras, but be careful when selecting one

When buying a used camera, you need to make sure that you will be getting one that works well for the price that you pay for it. Buying a used camcorder can be a great way to save money and still get a quality camera; shop around and find a lightly used and cared for piece of equipment.

One thing you should look for when buying used is the type of warranty that the equipment has. The warranty on a new camcorder will cover the item for a year or more, but if you buy a used or refurbished camcorder from the manufacturer, the warranty may be cut to ninety days or less. The longer a warranty that you can receive for the item, the better off you will be. You may have the option to purchase an extended

Exterior Condition

- Check the cosmetic appearance of the exterior of the camcorder.

- Any scratches or dings may be a sign of a camcorder that has been used hard or in a careless way.

- Make sure all the screws that hold the case on are there and securely fastened.

- Peeling stickers or lettering that has worn away may be due to normal use and is not necessarily a problem.

Lens Condition

- Inspect the lens for any scratches.

- If a clear filter is installed, it shows that the previous owner took good care not to damage the lens.

- Inspect the threads near the lens to make sure they are not stripped or damaged.

- Breathe gently on the lens to fog it up so you can see dust particles, fingerprints, and scratches. Make sure the fog clears evenly.

warranty, but the price of this extended warranty is often not worth the extra price.

The price that a seller asks for a used camcorder can be a good indication of what condition it is in. You shouldn't purchase a camcorder if the seller asks for 80 percent of the price of a new one. If the price is less than half of what a new camera costs it can be a sign that the used version is in bad condition or, worse, broken.

Buying a used camera from a private seller on an auction site like eBay is often the best way to go. Check the seller's ratings and be sure you are able to return the camera if it is not in the condition described in the auction listing.

Dead Pixels

- Dead pixels are tiny squares, usually white or black, that do not move. They cannot be removed by cleaning the lens or viewfinder.

- You may be able to deal with a dead pixel near the edge of the screen, but dead pixels near the center can be very irritating and debilitating.

- The only way to fix a dead pixel is to replace the imaging sensor.

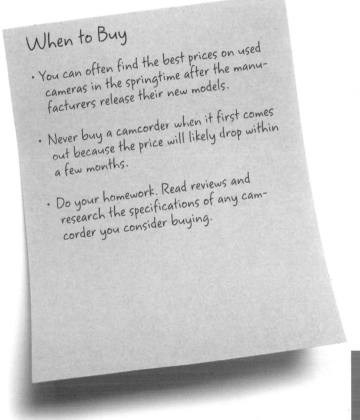

When to Buy

- You can often find the best prices on used cameras in the springtime after the manu- facturers release their new models.

- Never buy a camcorder when it first comes out because the price will likely drop within a few months.

- Do your homework. Read reviews and research the specifications of any cam- corder you consider buying.

HIGH-DEFINITION VIDEO CAMERAS
Buying a camera with HD capability is the right way to go

High definition (HD) will be the number one viewing medium for the foreseeable future. If you want your camera to be "future proof," then buying and using an HD camera is the way to go.

The picture quality that HD video cameras are capable of producing is incredible. HD cameras produce crisp and clear video that will look great on HDTV. Standard definition, by comparison, does not look very good on big screen HDTVs because the image is much smaller and must be stretched to fill the frame.

Standard-definition cameras are going by the wayside, and may in fact be obsolete in just a few short years. HD camcorders have many advantages over SD camcorders, including a wider choice of frame rates, low light capabilities, higher

Frame Rates

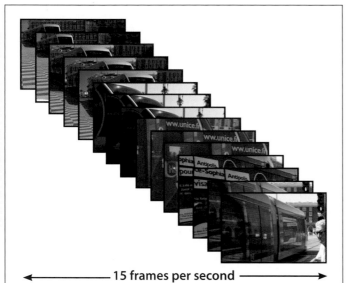

◄———— **15 frames per second** ————►

- The frame rate is the frequency at which frames in a video are displayed per second. In video, we measure frame rate with frames per second (fps).

- 60i (actually 59.94) is a frame rate that refers to 60 interlaced fields per second.

- Because the frames are interlaced there are actually only thirty full frames per second.

- 24p is a format that operates at twenty-four (or usually, 23.976fps) progressive frames per second.

Interlaced Video

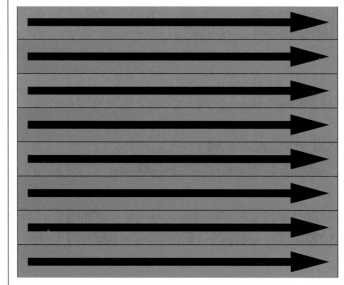

- The individual frames of an interlaced video sequence are created by scanning an image line by line.

- The process of interlacing divides this into odd and even lines called "fields" and then alternately refreshes them.

- The images containing the lines 1, 3, and 5 are called odd fields; the images containing the lines 2, 4, and 6 are called even fields. A consecutive pair of odd and even fields comprises a frame of interlaced video.

- Typical SD video is interlaced video, as is 1080i.

sound quality, and a better and larger picture, among other things. And, HD cameras still have the capability of recording in standard definition.

Prices for HD cameras are dropping lower by the day. In the coming years, as more and more people switch to HDTV and Blu-Ray players, manufacturers will stop producing standard-definition cameras altogether.

Progressive Video

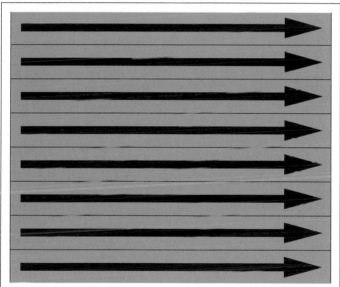

- Progressive scan video records each line of video in order, without skipping any lines.

- Progressive scan video typically looks better than interlaced with fast-motion video such as sports.

- A progressively scanned video image looks more stable than an interlaced one. Progressive scan shows fewer motion artifacts, such as jagged diagonal lines and movement in fine detail.

- Many camcorders allow you to shoot either progressive or interlaced video.

HD Formats

- Here are examples of popular formats and what they are commonly referred to as:

- 1080 60i (US Broadcast 1080i Video): 1920 x 1080 Resolution + 59.94 interlaced fields

- 720 60p (US Broadcast 720p Video): 1280 x 720 Resolution + 59.94 Progressive Frames

- 1080 24p: 1920 x 1080 Resolution + 23.98 Progressive Frames

- 720 24p: 1280 x 720 Resolution + 23.98 Progressive Frames

CAMERAS

CAMERA SETTINGS

When you're ready, turn off automatic mode and use manual settings for more control

As you get more comfortable with your camera, you will eventually want greater control over your image than what the automatic mode has to offer. Before you switch to full manual mode, you must first know what the automatic controls do and when they do it so you can determine when you want to take over the reins.

Professionals prefer to shoot in manual mode; however, many consumer level camcorders do not offer full manual controls. Instead they offer a cross between automatic and manual mode called AE mode. AE modes will make all of the necessary settings to shutter speed, aperture, and focusing for a variety of indoor and outdoor situations.

Exposure

- Exposure is the amount of light that is allowed to fall upon the image sensor.

- Generally, the camcorder's automatic exposure does a good job of determining the correct setting, but there are times when the camcorder gets fooled by uneven lighting conditions.

- Uneven lighting can cause high contrast between areas. Shadows may lack detail and be completely black (underexposed). Other times, bright areas in an image may appear completely white and "blown out" (overexposed).

Shutter Speed

- In video, shutter speed refers to the length of time that a single frame is exposed for.

- Shutter speed is measured in fractions of a second. A speed of 1/60 means that the shutter is open for one sixtieth of a second.

- Increasing the shutter speed allows you to capture fast-moving objects without causing motion blur.

- Increasing shutter speed limits the amount of light you allow in, so you may also have to increase the exposure.

One of the most commonly used AE modes is the sports mode. This mode is great for shooting fast-moving objects. It reduces blur by setting the shutter speed as high as possible, then adjusts the exposure level accordingly.

Portrait mode increases the shutter speed and opens the aperture to create a shallower depth of field that is desirable in portrait shots.

Shooting outdoors at a beach or a snowy location can cause problems for a camcorder's exposure. The camcorder will set the exposure too low and your images will turn out too dark.

The "surf and snow" or "beach and snow" mode adjusts the exposure for a more accurate image.

When shooting in low light on an automatic setting, your camcorder will try to keep the image as light as possible. There may be times when this is not desirable and you want to keep the image dark. The "sunset," "fireworks," or "candle" settings adjust the average tonal setting to keep the dark part of the image dark.

Landscape mode ensures that the camera focuses on distant objects and is useful when shooting through windows.

White Balance

- The auto-white balance on most camcorders is not particularly reliable in many situations and it is usually easier to perform this function manually.

- To manually set the white balance, first point the camcorder at a pure white object, such as a piece of computer paper. Activate the white balance by pressing the button for white balance or choose the white balance in the option menu.

- After a few seconds the camcorder will adjust the colors and your white balance will be set.

Focus

- Autofocus works by focusing the lens automatically, usually on the subject in the center of the viewfinder.

- Autofocus works well for fast shooting, but has many limitations.

- Using manual focus allows you to focus on exactly what you want.

- To set manual focus, zoom all the way in on the subject, focus on the subject, and then zoom back out. This will ensure your subject stays in focus throughout the zoom range.

CAMERAS

FUTURE CAMCORDERS
The future is here, but what will come next?

As technology continues to advance, manufacturers will likely strive to build even better quality hybrid photo/video cameras.

Camcorders have had the ability to shoot still photos for years but have done so poorly. Point and shoot cameras regularly offer video recording but fail to match the quality and features of a dedicated video camcorder. DSLR (digital single-lens reflex) cameras that record video are still relatively new,

but they offer the potential to capture video and still images with equal aptitude.

With their larger sensors and shallow depth of field, DSLRs can produce cinematic video unrivaled by any handheld camcorder. The technology is still new, so DSLR video cameras have serious limitations. As more and more models come out, we are likely to see prices come down and the

DSLR Video

- The first DSLR video cameras were the Nikon D90 and Canon 5DMKII, both introduced in 2008.

- Today there are quite a few VDSLRs on the market and several more planned for release. Their prices range from $600 at the base up to over $5,000.

- The low light capabilities, the ability to have extremely shallow depth of field, and the interchangeable lenses are a couple of the bigger advantage of using DSLR for video over a camcorder.

Flip Cams

- Pocket-style camcorders, such as the very popular Flip video camcorder, are expected to grow in the future.

- You should expect to see this style of camcorders debut with increased image and sound quality.

- Pocket camcorders will likely use wireless technology for sharing and uploading videos.

- Pocket-style camcorders pride themselves on being easy to use, so manual settings may be reserved for higher-end models.

negative issues addressed. DSLR video cameras will continue to push the limit and change people's perceptions on prosumer video.

The world of digital video is always changing, and it is impossible to know exactly where it is headed. Prices will drop; image quality will keep increasing; and new and exciting features will be developed. Imagine a cell phone that has a camera on it with the capability to record video that rivals the quality from today's most expensive HD cameras. Exciting indeed!

RED ONE

- The RED ONE and other cameras come from the RED Digital Cinema Camera company, which produces digital cinematography cameras for professional use.

- RED ONE is capable of recording at resolutions up to 4096 horizontal by 2304 vertical pixels.

- Academy Award–winning director Steven Soderbergh has already shot four feature films with the RED ONE.

- More directors are sure to follow his lead in the future and make the gradual switch from film to digital.

3D Camcorders

- Some studios and directors are predicting that 3D movies will be the third big innovation in filmmaking, after sound and color.

- As TV manufacturers begin to develop televisions capable of displaying 3D images, camcorder manufacturers will follow suit in develop-

ing camcorders capable of shooting in 3D.

- These camcorders will initially be very expensive, but become more affordable over time like all technology.

CAMERAS

TRIPODS

If you are serious about good-quality videos, a tripod is a necessity

The most important piece of equipment you can use to improve your video quality is a tripod. Anyone serious about good-quality camera work must understand the importance of using one. Almost all types of video work will require a tripod, so you must learn to use one.

Carbon fiber tripods are very light and they are the best at damping vibrations. They are also the most expensive. Plastic models are the lightest and least stable type. Metal tripods are very stable but they can be heavy.

A light, cheap, flimsy tripod can cause a lot of frustration and actually hurt your image quality. Buy a sturdy tripod that is good at dampening out vibrations. Spending a little more money to get a sturdy and stable tripod is worth it. Buying a tripod is a long-term investment.

Tripod Head

- Ball head tripods use ball and socket joints similar to the ones in your shoulders to allow the camera to move on all axes of rotation from a single point.

- Pan-tilt heads are the most common type of tripod head. They have separate adjustments for the pan and tilt usually in the form of handles that you unscrew to loosen.

- Your camcorder will attach to the head with a quick release plate with a thumb screw that fits into your camcorder.

Tripod Legs

- Inexpensive tripods will have legs made of cheap aluminum tubing and rubber feet that are not very sturdy.

- Quality, sturdy legs are usually heavier, although some tripods use composite materials such as carbon fiber to reduce weight.

- Tripod legs come in a variety of different heights. Try to use a tripod that is capable of going at least a little bit above your eye level.

Once you have a suitable tripod, the next step is to use it. Using a tripod often to steady your shots will make a world of difference in the watchability of your videos.

Tripod Operation

Monopod

- Spread the legs of the tripod and extend them to your desired height. Make sure you are able to move around comfortably without the legs getting in your way.

- Adjust the pan/tilt handle on the head to the angle you want. Use your right hand to control camera movement with the tripod handle and your left to operate the camera functions.

- Some camera operators prefer not to use the handle and instead control camcorder movement with their right hand on the camera itself.

- A monopod is basically a single legged tripod that gives the operator increased stability by supporting the weight of the camera.

- They are easier to carry and use than tripods, but they are not able to support a camera independently.

- Leaning against a wall or tree and using a monopod creates a bipod, which further helps with stabilization.

- Monopods can also be used as chest or belt pod by resting the base against your body to allow for movement.

LENS FILTERS

Using a filter in the right situation can dramatically improve your video image

Lens filters are pieces of glass that attach onto the threads on the end of your camcorder lens. Filters help you control color, composition, and add special effects to your video. These filters also have their own threads so you can stack more than one on top of each other to produce a stronger effect. They come in a variety of sizes to fit most camcorders and in

different strengths. The higher the number, the stronger the filter and the more it will affect your image.

The UV filter is the most commonly used filter for video work. It is the cheapest and most basic filter and should be the first one you buy. UV filters reduce the ultraviolet light coming into your lens and also reduce haze. More importantly,

Neutral Density Filter

Polarizing Density Filter

- The neutral density (ND) filter is used to limit the amount of light that can pass through the lens without influencing color or contrast.

- ND filters reduce overexposure and achieve a balanced image when filming in bright sunlight conditions.

- Neutral density filters are represented by optical density value. The higher the OD value, the stronger the effect. The most popular ND filters are ND 0.3, 0.6, and 0.9.

- Polarizing density filters change how your camera sees reflections and glare. As a result, these filters also have the ability to change the vibrancy of some colors.

- Polarizing density filters can make the sky appear much more vibrant. For best results, move the camera around so the sun is ninety degrees from the subject.

- You can minimize reflections in glass, screens, and water by using a polarizing density filter and shooting at an angle between thirty-five and sixty degrees from the reflecting element.

they protect your lens from getting scratched, smudged, or cracked. You should keep your UV filter permanently attached to your camcorder. It is much cheaper to replace a filter than it is to replace a lens or camcorder.

Many of the effects that you achieve with lens filters can be done in post-production with specialized software, but using filters on your camera upfront will generally result in a better overall image quality.

Day-for-night Filter

- Using a day-for-night filter allows you to shoot expensive and challenging night scenes during the day.

- The day-for-night filter creates a night effect by adding a bluish lavender tone to the video footage. The lens also has a low contrast element, which reduces the ability to see detail.

- To get the best results when using the day-for-night filter, avoid shooting the sky and adjust the exposure to make the image darker.

Assorted Filters

- Diffusion filters soften the subject in focus and smooth out textured surfaces.

- Mist filters are often used to create a dreamlike feel to your scenes.

- There are other special effect filters you can use such as star filters, center spot filters, and split field filters.

- These special effects filters have their uses, but it is usually better to add effects in post-production.

LENS ATTACHMENTS
When your camcorder lens just won't cut it, screw on a lens attachment

Unlike 35mm SLR photography cameras and professional broadcast cameras, most camcorders are not made for changing the lens. Instead, they come with a permanently affixed, built-in lens that lets you zoom in and out. The built-in lens does the job for most types of shooting; however, there will be many times when the built-in lens doesn't fit the bill.

It can be frustrating when you can't frame everything you want to shoot into one shot. This is the perfect time to use a wide-angle lens adapter. It will expand the standard horizontal and vertical field of view that your camcorder is able to see, enabling you to fit much more into a shot. These lenses work great for capturing wide panoramic outdoor images as well.

Camera Lens Threads

- On the front of your camcorder near the lens, there are a series of grooves, or threads, where you can screw in various accessories.

- These threads are measured in millimeters and come in varying sizes. Your cam-corder will usually have the size printed on it near the lens. If it doesn't, check the owner's manual.

- Match the thread size of the filter or lens adapter to your camcorder's thread size for a perfect fit.

Wide-angle Lens

- Adding a wide-angle lens adapter allows you to fit more peripheral information into your shot.

- Be wary, however: A wide-angle lens can cause a certain amount of distortion. It can make the distance between objects seem extended. It also makes objects close to you seem larger and can make straight lines in the frame appear to be slightly bent.

- A fisheye lens is an extremely wide lens that gives a unique, distorted image for special effects.

Wide-angle lenses have their limitations, however. At their widest setting, they may introduce an unacceptable amount of distortion. You won't be able to zoom once your wide-angle lens is attached unless you have a "zoom through" type lens. These lenses allow you to use the zoom and the lens at the same time without causing distortion.

Telephoto lenses do the opposite of wide-angle lenses. With a telephoto lens attached to your original lens, you can zoom into objects much farther away than you traditionally can with your standard camcorder lens. Telephoto lenses

work great for shooting wildlife or sports events when you aren't able to get close to the action.

Depth of field (DOF) 35mm adapters are the most complex and difficult to use lenses that you can add to your camcorder. They allow you to use 35mm photography lenses as an attachment to your camcorder. Another specialty lens, a macro lens, is like a magnifying glass for your camcorder. It allows you to get extremely close to very tiny objects.

Telephoto Lens

- When you can't get close enough to what you want to shoot with your camcorder's optical zoom, you can increase the zoom range by adding a telephoto lens.

- A 2x telephoto lens will make the images appear twice as close as they appear without the lens.

- Telephoto lenses restrict the amount of light that can get to the camcorder's imaging sensor, so they are best used outdoors in situations with plenty of light.

DOF Adapter

- A DOF 35mm adapter allows you to use 35mm photography lenses on your camcorder.

- The DOF adapter is made up of four parts: a macro lens, an optional plano-convex lens, a translucent focusing screen, and a photographic lens of the user's choice.

- Using a DOF adapter can make your video footage look like it was shot on film by softening the image and giving it a shallow depth of field.

CAMERA RIGS

Produce fluid camera movement when using these stabilizers and camera rigs

Beginning shooters use camera supports only when forced to, whereas the pros are the opposite, going handheld only when no better camera support will work. The three main types of camera supports are tripods, stabilizers, dollies, and booms. Each type has its pros and cons and all of them can cost a lot of money. Understanding these camera supports

will help you pick the right one for the job.

Steadicam stabilizers produce handheld shots that look almost like dolly shots, except they can go places where dolly track could never be set up. Although simple stabilizers for lightweight camcorders are no more expensive than comparable tripods, the rigs required for professional-size cameras

The Steadicam

- The Steadicam is a device that functions as a stabilizing mount for a motion-picture camera.

- By utilizing a Steadicam, it is possible to capture action without causing unintentional jerky movement or lack of focus in the shot.

- The Steadicam can take on a couple of different forms, depending on the type of camera in use and the environment in which the camera is utilized.

The Jib

- The jib, or camera crane, is a mechanical device that is used to hold a camera on an extended arm.

- When using a jib, the camera is able to move from one location to another while zooming out, rising,

or descending at the same time, producing incredible footage.

- A jib comes in many different sizes and is often mounted on a tripod, dolly, or similar support.

can run into the tens of thousands of dollars.

Dollies come in two basic types: floor models and track models. The types of dollies that you can use vary so much that some can be packed in a couple of canvas bags (track and all) while others need a truck. Versatile floor types roll on tires that are smooth and silent and can change direction completely in the middle of a shot.

Track dollies use wheels that ride on rails. They take much longer to set up because you have to build them like toy train layouts, but they are unparalleled in their smoothness across all kinds of uneven terrain. The tracks also make it easy to repeat moves exactly for additional takes.

If your budget doesn't include all of the equipment you want, or if you are the type who enjoys the challenge of building, how about a DIY project? The Internet has lots of resources; check the resources section for links. There are plans to design and build everything from tripods to stabilization devices. Some people get a sense of satisfaction from making a rig themselves.

Camera Dolly

- A camera dolly is a specialized piece of film equipment designed to create smooth camera movements.

- The camera dolly may be used as a shooting platform on any surface but is often raised onto track, to create smooth tracking shots.

- Dolly track is usually steel or aluminum, but lightweight plastic and PVC versions of track are also available and can be used with light-weight dolly systems.

Types of Jibs

- When a filmmaker wants to have extreme height and reach, he chooses a large jib controlled from the rear.

- Since the camera operator is often not able to use the camera's controls directly or look through the camera's viewfinder, a jib is often used with a remote camera control for focus and zoom and with a portable video monitor.

- When a filmmaker wants subtle movements in the two- to eight-foot range, the best tool is a front-operated jib. These smaller, lightweight jib arms are not only easier to use, but more affordable and quicker to set up.

BUILDING UP YOUR EQUIPMENT

You don't want to find yourself without the necessary equipment while on set

To get the most out of your system, buy individual components that are similar in quality, capability, and cost. Shooting an important project with your new $1500 camcorder and a $50 tripod will be a very disappointing experience. It also makes little sense to use a $2300 tripod with a $600 basic camcorder. Choose your equipment so that each piece

matches in quality and compatibility and complements the other parts of the system.

It is also very important to stay within your budget and buy only what you need. The price of a piece of equipment has very little to do with whether it will satisfy your production needs. Though the more expensive model may be a better

Generator

- When shooting on location you may not have an available power source to power your lights, camera, and other equipment. In this case, your only option may be to use a generator.

- Generators can be very noisy. You should run about

100 to 200 feet of extension cords, so the sound from the generator will dissipate before reaching your audio equipment.

- Buy a generator that provides enough power for your lights, but also runs quietly.

Apple Boxes and Sandbags

- The sandbag is a heavy bag full of sand that is used on a film set to secure the base of tripods and c-stands (light stands).

- Apple boxes are wooden boxes of varying sizes with holes on each end used for a wide variety of tasks on a film set such as propping

up furniture, leveling light stands, or for temporary seats, workbenches, and stepladders.

- The different sizes are Full Apple (8x20x12 feet), Half Apple (4x20x12), Quarter Apple (2x20x12 feet), and Pancake (1x20x12 feet).

piece of equipment, it may not provide the best bang for the buck.

For example, a $300 wireless microphone system is usually better than a $50 system. It provides a better frequency response, higher-quality audio, and a greater operating range. A $2000 wireless microphone system may be even better than the $300 system—but not worth the extra $1700 to meet your specific needs.

It's also important to plan your video system with the future in mind. The more video production you do, the better your skills become. Better skills often lead to a desire for better, more sophisticated equipment. There will also be a greater demand for your skills. Unless you have an incredible amount of money or win the lottery, you won't be able to completely replace your current system. Build your new system one step at a time, improving one component of the system at each step. You should look at every purchase in terms of how the individual piece of equipment will complement the present and future equipment.

Gaffers' Tape and Clothespins

- Gaffers' tape is a strong cotton cloth pressure-sensitive tape that adheres strongly but can be removed cleanly without leaving a residue.

- It is often used to secure cables to the stage floor, to temporarily fix broken equipment, and to lay blocking markers for actors.

- Clothespins or "C47s" are commonly used on film sets to attach a color correction gel or diffusion to the barn doors on a light.

Multi-tools

- A multi-tool has numerous tools that fold out from its handles. They generally have pliers, a knife, a saw, a small ruler, Phillips and flathead screwdrivers, and a bottle opener.

- The cheapest multi-tools break easily, so it is better to invest in a decent one.

Leatherman and Gerber are excellent brand names for multi-tools.

- It is also a good idea to keep a flashlight handy.

- Keep these items with you at all times when filming; you will use them more than you realize.

MORE EQUIPMENT
You never know what you may need while filming

Investing in video equipment and other filmmaking peripherals can be costly. It is always a smart idea to invest in high-quality equipment so it can be used for a long time.

There are many ways that you can acquire or purchase the equipment you need. If you know a local store catering to film production equipment and accessories, visit that store and see what they have to offer. In a store you can get the

firsthand feel and experience of a piece of equipment. You can test out the gear and check right away for any defects or things about the item that you don't like. You can also negotiate a lower price if needed.

Getting your hands on the gear you intend to buy is especially important if the item you are looking to buy is expensive. You may want to look into renting the gear for a day in order

Camera Cases

- Every filmmaker needs carrying cases to travel from location to location. They also offer a safe place to keep your equipment when you are not using it.

- There are soft cases and hard cases.

- Hard cases offer a little bit

more protection against damage but are heavy, cumbersome, and can be difficult to pack.

- Soft camera cases are easier to pack and extremely versatile. Most have movable dividers that can be rearranged or removed.

Lens Cleaner

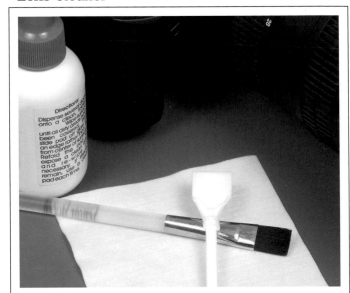

- Small amounts of dust on a lens will not greatly affect image quality, but fingerprints and oily smudges can leave prints on the surface of your lens that will distort your image.

- With a soft brush, carefully brush away any dust and

dirt particles that may be on your camera lens.

- If soft brushing doesn't remove the dirt, dampen a lens tissue with lens cleaner, and gently rub the lens in a circular motion.

to put it through its paces in a real world environment.

On paper, a particular piece of gear may look amazing, but real world use truly proves its value. Simply put, technical specs do not make a great product. That's why research is so vital. Read trade magazines, browse Internet forums, and read user reviews online.

Every movie is different, so it's very difficult to determine exactly everything you might need to produce a particular movie. However, all movies tend to have the same basic minimum requirements. The casual shooter only needs two basic pieces of equipment—a camcorder and tripod—but good video productions start with solid, smooth video, quality audio, and good lighting that matches the mood or style of the production. Once you have a video production system that provides all of these essentials, you can begin adding other pieces of equipment as needed.

Clapperboard

- A clapperboard or slate is a device with a hinged arm that swings ninety degrees to make a loud crack sound that is recorded by the camera before a scene starts.

- The main purpose of a clapperboard is to help you sync your sound to your video if you're using an external recorder, but it can also be important in logging your footage and keeping your project organized.

- Today, electronic clappers and synchronization are often used instead of the old-fashioned clapperboard.

Advice on Lens Cleaning

- Every cleaning carries with it a very small risk of scratching the lens or causing other problems. The best way to keep lenses and filters clean is not to let them get dirty in the first place.

- Never drip lens cleaner directly on a lens. It can easily seep behind lens elements and create a major problem.

- A small amount of dust is unlikely to affect image quality, so don't become too obsessive about lens cleaning. The marginal improvement in picture quality is not worth the risk of permanent lens damage that can happen from cleaning.

THE IMPORTANCE OF LIGHTING
The way a film is lit plays an important part in the storytelling process

Besides your camera, lighting is the one factor that will determine the overall image quality of your video. For professional results, give your lighting the same careful consideration that you would give in selecting your actors, music, and script. The way you light the set and actors shapes the way the audience receives your message. It sets the mood of the scene and sets the tone of the environment. Proper lighting will not only give you saturated colors, but will also help create depth of field, setting your video apart from the crowd.

Digital video cameras can be more light-sensitive than most film stocks, and therefore require less light to be cast on the same image. Digital video has a low color resolution, so

KNACK DIGITAL MOVIEMAKING

Poor Lighting

- Video shot with poor lighting results in a muddy, grainy, indistinct, almost colorless image.

- Poor lighting can make the most expensive professional video camera look inferior.

- Modern cameras shoot well in a variety of lighting conditions, except in very low light or strong contrast situations.

- The only way to fix low light is to add more light while shooting.

Over-Lit Image

- Video that was shot with too much light results in a whitish, washed-out, faded-looking image.

- An over-lit image will be overexposed.

- Some video cameras have a function called Zebra Stripes. When activated, diagonal lines appear on the LCD screen or viewfinder across any part of the image that approaches overexposure.

- There is little you can do to fix overexposed video in post-production, so be careful when shooting in bright areas.

it is important to know how to filter and white balance your camcorder.

All light sources have a distinct color that is rated by the Kelvin temperature scale. Kelvin is a unit of measurement used to describe the hue of a specific light source. The higher the Kelvin value of the light source, the closer the light's color output will be to actual sunlight. The color temperature of a light does not refer to the heat of light, but rather the color of the light that we see. Indoor light is around 3200K, outdoor light is 5600K, fluorescent light around 4200K. The white balance setting on a camcorder will have a great effect on how light is viewed on video. If your camera is set for daylight, it will see indoor lighting as orange. If your camera is set for indoors, the scene out your window will look very blue. Shooting under fluorescent light gives your video a greenish cast. These problems can be avoided if you white balance your camera each time you film under a new light source.

Contrast Ratio

- Contrast ratio refers to the brightest part of the shot compared to the darkest.

- While the human eye can perceive contrast ratios over a range of 400:1 to 10,000:1, the maximum contrast ratio a video system can handle is about 30:1.

- When there is too much contrast in a video image, the camera commonly reads the light parts but turns the dark burns into pure black, or reads the darker parts but turns the lightest parts into pure white.

Well-Lit Image

- When lighting for a shot like the one pictured above, make sure your subject is brighter than your background.

- Take your time in lighting a scene; very little can be done to correct bad lighting during the editing process.

- A well-lit video will be devoid of distracting shadows, image noise, and blotchy color.

SOFT LIGHT VERSUS HARD LIGHT
Every light source is inherently hard or soft

All light sources can be defined as either hard or soft. Hard light travels mostly straight in direction and casts distinct shadows, while soft light is diffused light that produces soft shadows. Whether light falling on a subject is hard or soft depends on one thing: the relative sizes of the light source and subject. A large light source will wrap light around a small subject, filling shadows and lowering contrast. A small light source will direct light onto a large subject, creating hard shadows and high contrast.

When hard light is used to illuminate a face, imperfections in the skin stand out. This doesn't mean hard light is a bad light. Rather, it can be successfully used to bring out the details in an object or to give your subject a dramatic, aggressive, manly look. Outside of these stylized lighting effects, hard

Soft Light

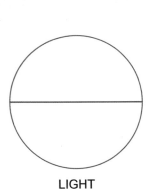

LIGHT   SUBJECT

- There are two main factors that determine the softness of a light source: distance and size.

- The closer the light source, the softer it becomes. The larger the source, the softer it becomes.

- The angle between the illuminated object and the length of the light source can also determine how soft light will be. The larger this angle is, the softer the light source.

Soft Light Portrait

- Soft light tends to hide surface irregularities and details and is usually more flattering than hard light, particularly for women.

- Notice the lack of contrast and shadows on the model's face in the picture above. The light seems to wrap around her face, from all sides.

- The photo was lit using a light placed very close to the model's face diffused by a large umbrella.

light is rarely used to light an actor's face.

Using soft or diffused light is one of the most natural and warm ways to light an actor. Soft light creates fewer shadows, making the actor's skin look smoother. Using soft light to illuminate objects minimizes surface detail.

The most realistic lighting is often a combination of hard and soft light. This type of light is more in line with how we see people in everyday life.

MAKE IT EASY

The sun is a very large light source, but from our perspective, it appears small. This fact makes the sun a hard light. On a sunny day, the sun will cast a very sharp shadow across an object. However, a layer of clouds will diffuse the sun's light, casting less shadows and making it a soft light source. This is why many photographers would rather shoot outside on a cloudy day than on a sunny one.

Hard Light

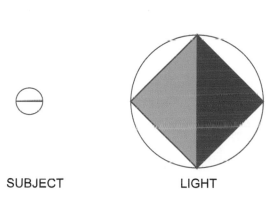

SUBJECT   LIGHT

- Hard light comes from a small light source.

- The light rays emitted from a hard light are coherent or parallel, resulting in a light with a hard, crisp, sharply defined appearance that casts a clearly defined shadow.

- Using hard light casts dark shadows and produces high contrast video with deep blacks and bright highlights.

Hard Light Portrait

- The shadows created by hard lights enhance the model's facial features. The image is not as flat and has a better sense of depth.

- Although not evident in the above photo, hard light tends to show imperfections in the subject's complexion.

- Hard light can be used to emphasize harshness or starkness. For instance, a grizzled old sheriff may be shot with hard light.

- Black and white is classic for hard light; the strong contrast and lack of details in the shadows will work well together.

LIGHTING EQUIPMENT
Set your project apart with the right equipment

Deciding on the proper lighting equipment to use can be difficult, especially with the wide variety of equipment and costs. The most important thing is to choose a light or lighting kit that is portable and flexible. Every lighting situation will be different; having a flexible kit will allow you to work around any obstacle.

Whether you're buying one light, several lights, or a kit, the next step is to decide what kind of bulb you want to purchase. Incandescent bulbs are like the common household bulb. The heating of a tungsten filament creates the light, which results in a warmer color temperature than daylight. Incandescent bulbs are the least expensive bulb type, but they don't create a lot of light, and you need to replace them frequently.

Halogen bulbs are similar to incandescent bulbs but are

On-camera Lights

- On-camera lights sit on top of your camera and shine light onto the middle of the subject's face.

- On-camera lights are usually very small hard lights that throw an intense harsh light toward your subject.

- Although these kinds of lights have their limitations, they can be very useful for on-the-fly shooting when you find yourself unable to use a full light kit.

Spotlights

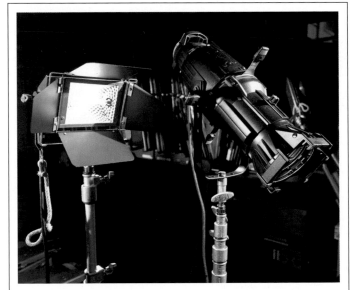

- Spotlights—or "spots," as they're sometimes called—have strong beams that can be focused. The light beam can be narrowed or widened by moving the lamp forward or back in its housing.

- Because you can soften spotlights, they are the most versatile lighting instruments, suitable for key, fill, rim, and background lighting.

- Conversely, floodlights are large lights that are basically the opposite of spots.

filled with halogen gas. The added gas allows for a brighter-burning light and an extended lifespan. The color temperature is closer to daylight than incandescent bulbs. Halogen bulbs are inexpensive, but they create a lot of heat and use more power than regular bulbs.

Due to their tendency to flicker and emit a greenish hue, fluorescent bulbs were not used for lighting film and video until recently. In fact, these bulbs did not become popular until manufacturers developed fluorescent lights that were flicker free and came in both daylight and tungsten balanced bulbs. Like incandescents, fluorescent bulbs cast a soft light and use less power, but they also do not give off as much light as other bulb types. Other less frequently used but still important bulbs include LED and HMI.

Softbox

- A softbox is a box that fits over a lamp that has black sides, with a reflective interior and a translucent front where light passes through.

- Softboxes are designed to soften the high contrast light from small light sources. They produce a light that is even and soft, making them ideal for lighting faces.

- By adding a softbox to your lighting gear, you double the use of your lights because they now can be used either as soft or hard lights.

Color Gels

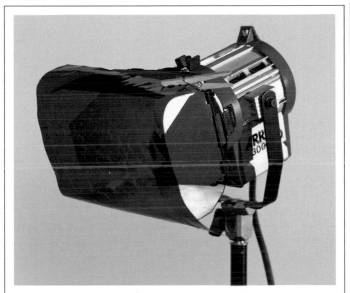

- Gels are translucent sheets of heat-resistant material that are placed between a light source and the subject being lit to color light and for color correction. Color correction gels are most commonly used to convert the color temperature of tungsten light to daylight.

- Diffusion gels diffuse the light without changing the color temperature.

- Neutral density (ND) gels dim or reduce the output of a light.

- Color gels come in an endless variety of colors and are used for lighting accents.

THREE-POINT LIGHTING
Use this technique to get an even light for interviews

The three-point lighting technique is one of the oldest methods used for lighting a scene. The technique uses three lights called the key light, fill light, and back light. It is a simple but versatile system that forms the basis of most lighting used in film. Once you understand three-point lighting, you are on your way to understanding all film lighting.

The three-point system is most often used to light interviews.

By using three separate positions for lights, you are able to illuminate the interview subject however you want while controlling or eliminating the shading and shadows produced by direct lighting.

The key light highlights the form and dimension of the subject. It is the main light in the three-point system and creates the overall look of your lighting. Traditionally, the key light

KNACK DIGITAL MOVIEMAKING

The Key Light

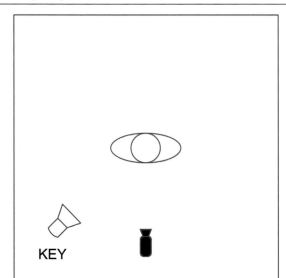

- The key light is placed between a thirty- and forty-five-degree angle from either the left or the right of the camera.

- It should be elevated to about thirty to forty-five degrees above the subject.

- The key light should be in the middle of the hard-to-soft light range.

- The hardness, softness, horizontal angle, and vertical angle can all be altered to produce different lighting effects.

Fill Light

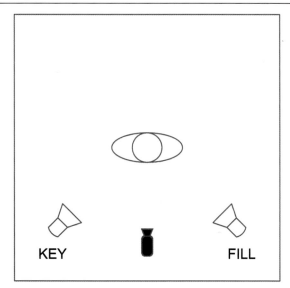

- Ideally, the fill light should be about ninety degrees away from the key light and placed just above camera height.

- The fill light should be softer than the key light so it partially fills in the shadows created by the key.

- The key/fill light difference helps provide much of the illusion of three dimensions on a two-dimensional medium.

has been a hard light, such as a spot, but in the last few years more and more filmmakers have been using a soft light as the key. It is up to you to decide which type of key will do the best job in getting your desired look.

Place the key on the subject's better side. It will emphasize the positive and downplay the negative facial features. Be consistent in your key lighting. If two people sit next to each other, key them both from the same side.

Fill light is useful in video production as a way to lighten the dark areas produced by the key light. The fill light should be

dimmer and more diffused than your key light source. The back light goes behind your subject and separates him or her from the background. The back light shouldn't be as bright as your key light.

Back Light

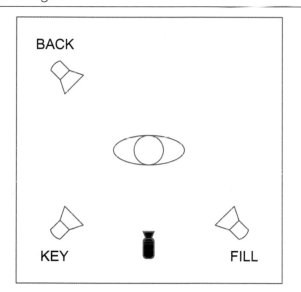

- The back light should be positioned a few feet above the subject's head, either directly behind the subject or off to the side.

- The function of the back light is to separate the subject from the background by creating a subtle rim of light around the subject.

- Make sure the light itself cannot be seen in the frame or that light shining into the camera lens does not produce camera flare.

- The back light is also known as the rim, hair light, or shoulder light.

Four-point Lighting

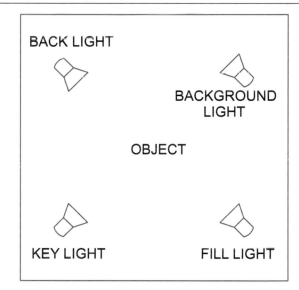

- Add a background light to turn a three-point setup into a four-point setup. The background light adds depth and separation from the subject.

- If the background has detail or texture, you will want to put the background light

on the same side of the subject as the key.

- Any type of light can be used as a background light if its lighting is even across the background; it does not hit the central subject matter; and it shines at the appropriate intensity.

SETTING THE MOOD WITH LIGHT

Evoke a certain feeling in the audience by designing creative lighting setups

Hollywood films have lighting designers who work closely with directors to build a lighting scheme that adds to the drama and emotion of a scene. Lighting can make a scene feel happy, sad, mysterious, or even dangerous.

The quality of the overall lighting scheme and its effect on mood is often dependent on the relationship between the key and fill lights. If they are about the same intensity, the scene will be perceived as bright and happy. As the fill becomes less and less intense, the scene becomes more dramatic. The back light also plays a role. The more intense the back light, the more dramatic the effect.

Changing the angle, intensity, and color of your lights can

High-key Lighting

- A high-key lit scene features overall bright lighting that is evenly lit and free from dark shadows.

- High-key lighting tends to be cheerful, expansive, and energetic, which is why it's often used for sitcoms, comedies, and musicals.

- To achieve a high-key look, make sure that your background is almost as bright as your subjects, and that you fill in most shadows enough to reveal details in them.

Low-key Lighting

- A low-key lit scene will be mainly dark, with deep shadows and just a few areas accented with light.

- Low-key lighting can look intimate, dramatic, romantic, sad, or scary. It is most commonly used in drama, horror, and film noir genres.

- Low-key lighting requires only one key light that, optionally, can be controlled with additional fill light or a reflector.

dramatically alter the mood of a scene. For example: For a scene with a man proposing to his girlfriend, you would want to create a lighting scheme that brings about a warm and romantic feeling. You can achieve this by softening the shadows and changing the color of the lights to a warm gold, or a light pink. Lighting that same scene with a bright spotlight would ruin the mood and take away from the emotion you are trying to pass on to your audience.

•••••••••••• GREEN ● LIGHT ••••••••••••

Take note of the different lighting used in different places: in an office, at an expensive restaurant, in a bowling alley, etc. Observe what mood is created by the light; how that mood is created; and what it would take to replicate that scene. Evaluate the direction, the source, the quality, and the color of the light. When you come across a scene you like, take notes so that you can replicate it later.

High Contrast

- The mood in high- and low-key scenes is affected by the overall contrast. High-contrast light looks harsh, while low-contrast light produces a softer mood.

- High-contrast lighting is dominated by bright lines of light combined with dramatic dark areas.

- High-contrast scenes can look dreary, powerful, and gritty, while scenes with low contrast ratios can appear dreamy, or gloomy and depressed.

Color Hue

- Certain colors evoke specific feelings in people. The overall color of a scene can have a large emotional effect on the viewer.

- Adjusting a picture's hue is usually done in post-production, but often it can be easier to do on set using colored gels.

- The white balance on your camcorder can be manipulated to change the overall color of your footage. For example: Setting the white balance mode to tungsten will introduce a blue cast to your footage when shooting outdoors.

TIPS & TRICKS

Try these tips and tricks to improve your lighting design

To become skilled at lighting, you first must become comfortable using different lighting equipment and practice lighting scenes in a variety of conditions. The more lighting you do, the more shortcuts and tricks you'll learn that will help you light scenes efficiently and quickly.

First, monitor your lights as you set them up. Judging the lighting of a scene with just your eyes can get you into trouble.

A better idea is to use your camera's LCD screen or viewfinder to see exactly how the lighting is affecting the image. The video camera will see light differently than your eye does. As you adjust your lighting setup, keep coming back to check the LCD screen. This process moves a lot quicker with two people. If you have time, tape a short segment with the lighting setup and then play it back over a television monitor. This

Hardware Light

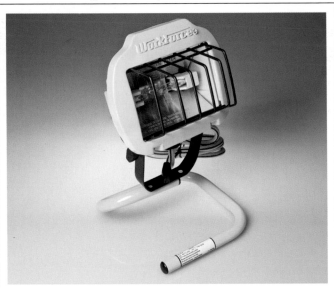

- A good cheap key light is a 500-watt tungsten work light, which can be found at hardware and car parts stores.

- They sometimes come with their own stands, but the stands tend to be a little short.

- The light from a work light is hard to control, so it's best to not aim them directly at your subject.

- Bouncing the light off of a wall or ceiling creates a nice soft light.

Chinese Lanterns

- Chinese lanterns or China balls are made of paper material that can be expanded into a ball with a bulb inside. They are an inexpensive, lightweight solution for lighting scenes.

- Using a regular 200-watt bulb inside a China lantern

- makes a great soft light for close-ups.

- China balls are cheap and well respected among pros. They can be seen providing soft light on guerilla shorts and high budget movies alike.

gives you a better idea of how your finished video will look and eliminates surprises in the editing room.

Your video should be lit shot by shot. This means that you need to reposition the lights whenever you relocate the camera. This is one reason films take so long to shoot. Try to schedule your camera shots for scenes so that you minimize the need to relocate lights and save some time.

Reflector Card

- A reflector or bounce board is a white or silver card used for soft indirect lighting of the subject by bouncing light off the card.

- Reflector boards are often used outdoors to bounce light from the sun onto a subject to provide a gentle brightening of shadow areas.

- Experiment with the light reflector to achieve the desired effect on your subject. Don't be afraid to try a variety of different techniques to achieve the desired lighting.

Extension Cords

- Every lighting kit should include a variety of heavy-weight extension cords. Get them in an assortment of lengths and buy a few more of them than you think you will need.

- Get extension cords that are a bright yellow, orange, or red color so they won't blend in with grass.

- Label the extension cords with your name so somebody doesn't walk off with one by mistake.

- Also make sure you have a power strip and a few ground-to-two-prong adapters.

83

THE IMPORTANCE OF SOUND

Often overlooked when filming, sound is just as important as the image on the screen

The importance of sound in film cannot be underestimated. A film's soundtrack can be just as important as, if not more important than, the images on the screen.

The soundtrack of a movie is composed of three main elements: the human voice, sound effects, and music. These three individual tracks must be mixed together to produce

the necessary emphasis, which, in turn, creates desired effects and adds to your story.

The use of sound is an important tool for drawing the audience into the film. The audience can hear dozens of distinct sounds all at the same time and separate and process them. Sound can consist of different layers without confusing an

Mood

- The sound in a film can convey different feelings of emotion and alter the mood of a scene.

- A video of a man/woman walking down the street with scary music in the background lets the audi-

ence know that something frightening may be about to happen.

- The same scene with happy music playing makes you feel like the character is in good spirits.

Elements of Sound

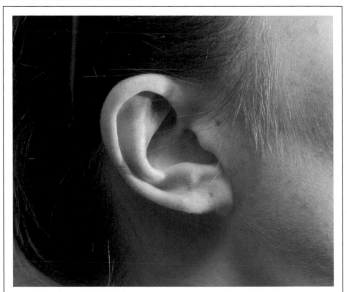

- The sound in a film is made up of three major elements: dialogue, music, and sound effects.

- The dialogue encompasses any spoken word by any character in your film, including conversations and narrations.

- Music makes up the score or soundtrack of your film. And sound effects make up a wide variety of other noises such as ambiance, explosions, and footsteps.

- These three elements must be mixed together in such a way that best aids the telling of your story.

audience, while different layers of pictures definitely would be confusing. Therefore, much more information can be transmitted from the filmmaker to the audience via sound than via picture.

Even in the silent film era, music was an important part of film. Showings of silent films almost always featured live music. Music was recognized as essential from the beginning. Movies were never meant to be watched in total silence. Instead, movies are supposed to mirror real life and real life always includes many sounds.

ZOOM

Audiences are more forgiving of poor-quality video than of poor-quality audio. No viewer will strain himself to hear your audio. While subpar-quality video can be written off as artistic, bad-quality audio cannot. *The Blair Witch Project* had relatively bad video quality, but because the sound quality was okay, the film was not hard to watch.

Sound versus Picture

- It has been said that between 50 and 90 percent of the audience's experience comes through a film's sound.

- It is easier for an audience to process multiple sounds in a movie than it is to process multiple images. If you try to watch a movie with the sound on mute, you quickly lose track of the storyline. If you watch a movie blindfolded, however, you will still be able to follow the story.

Synchronous versus Asynchronous

- Synchronous sound refers to all those audio elements that come from sources inside the world we see on the screen, including dialogue, doors slamming, footsteps, etc.

- Asynchronous sound refers to all those audio elements that come from outside of the fictional world we see on screen, including the musical score and sound effects.

SOUND

85

AUDIO WAVEFORMS

Learning the fundamentals of sound waves will help you work with them

To fully understand audio, you must have a firm grasp on how sound waves work. You need to be able to see the specific faces that each sound wave can have, based on three important characteristics: frequency, wavelength, and amplitude.

Sound waves are created by the vibration of an object, like the cone in a radio loudspeaker. When this force is exerted on an atom, it moves from its rest position and exerts a force on the adjacent particles. These adjacent particles are moved from their rest position and this continues throughout the room until the vibration reaches your eardrum. The vibrating air then causes the human eardrum to vibrate, which, in turn, the brain interprets as sound.

Amplitude

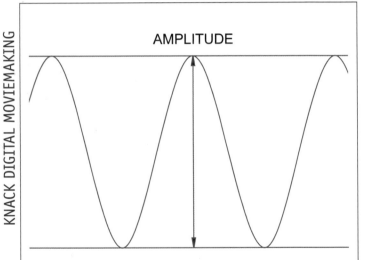

AMPLITUDE

- Amplitude is the measurement of the degree of change (positive or negative) in atmospheric pressure caused by sound waves.

- The more energy the sound wave has the louder the sound seems. You hear intensity as loudness.

- In digital audio waveforms, amplitude is displayed as the height of the wave.

- Acoustic Intensity is measured in decibels (dB). One decibel equals approximately the smallest difference in acoustic power the human ear can detect.

Wavelength

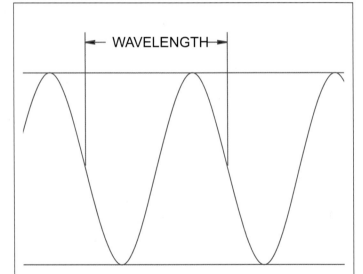

WAVELENGTH

- Wavelength is the spacing of the waves, or the distance between one point—or node—on a wave and the same point on the next wave.

- The differences in the pitch of the sound are caused by different spacing in the

- waves; the closer together the waves are, the higher the tone sounds.

- High frequency sounds have short wavelengths while low frequency sounds have long wavelengths.

Sound waves are often shown in a standard X (horizontal) versus Y (vertical) graph. The curves on this graph are known as the "waveform." The waveform graph is two-dimensional, but in reality sound waves are three-dimensional. They do not move in a line from left to right as shown in the graph; they move in all directions originating from the source. Sound waves move through air in much the same way as waves ripple on a pond. However, the two-dimensional graph is the best way to show how sound travels from one place to another.

ZOOM

Many sounds in film have become clichés over time that you should try to avoid. Any time an animal is shown in a movie it makes more noise than it normally ever would. Snakes make rattling noises, dogs bark, and cats meow. Bombs make a whistling sound when they fall from a plane. Urban areas constantly have police sirens in the background and country areas have cricket noises.

Audio Frequency

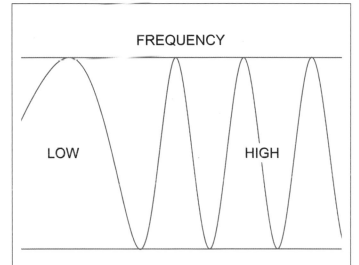

FREQUENCY

LOW   HIGH

- Frequency is the number of times one wavelength occurs in one second. Frequency is measured in hertz (Hz) or cycles per second (CPS).

- Higher frequencies are higher pitched. When you speak in a high-pitched voice, you are forcing your vocal cords to vibrate quickly.

- Humans can hear sounds ranging from 20 to about 20,000 hertz. 20Hz would sound like an extremely low-pitched organ while 20,000Hz would sound higher than the highest note on a violin.

Decibel Levels

- 194 dB: loudest sound possible

- 140 dB: short-term exposure to sounds at this volume can cause permanent damage

- 115 dB: volume of a loud rock concert

- 90-95 dB: sustained exposure to sounds at this volume may result in hearing loss

- 60-70 dB: normal conversation volume

- 30 dB: volume of a quiet library

SOUND

TYPES OF MICROPHONES
Add an external microphone to capture great sound

The built-in microphones that come on cameras have their limitations, so it's good to have additional external mics with you for added sound. There are more microphone options than any other type of camcorder accessory, including small clip-on "lavalier" mics that are great for interviews, stereo mics for recording ambiance, directional shotgun mics, large studio mics for recording voiceovers and instruments, and so on.

Microphones can be either wired or wireless. Wired mics are directly connected to the camcorder, thus limiting the distance from which you can record. Wireless microphones come with a receiver that is connected to the camcorder and a transmitter that is connected to the microphone. Wireless mics can be expensive; also, they sometimes have a limited range and may suffer from signal interference.

External Microphones

- When buying an external mic, first determine what type of microphone connection your camcorder has.

- Most consumer camcorders use a standard TRS (tip ring sleeve) ⅛ inch (3.5mm) mono or stereo microphone connection.

- Professional model cameras usually use XLR-type connections.

- The big advantage of XLR connections over TRS connections is that you can run longer cables from the camera to the mic without experiencing interference.

External Camera Microphone

- The most common type of external mic attaches to the top of the camcorder on its accessory shoe, a type of mounting found on some camcorders that supports additional devices such as microphones or lights.

- Camera noises and vibrations may be heard when using a camera-mounted external microphone. These can be eliminated by adding a shock mount.

- The shock mount will float your mic so that internal camera noises and vibrations don't work their way up to your microphone.

Microphones can be either omni-directional or uni-directional. Omni-directional mics record sounds in all directions from the microphone and are great for recording ambiance. Uni-directional mics, like shotgun mics, only record sounds from the direction in which they are pointed.

Cardoid microphones pick up a specific sound in one direction and record very little background noise. The supercardoid microphone eliminates even more background noise, particularly from directly behind the microphone. And the hypercardoid microphone eliminates more noise from the sides.

Shotgun Microphones

- Shotgun microphones are directional mics that only pick up sound in the direction in which they are pointed.

- Shotgun mics are the most common type of external microphones.

- Shotgun camcorder micro-phones can be mounted onto your camcorder or attached to a boom pole.

- Shotgun mics are much more sensitive than on-camera mics, and pick up better sound.

- Shotgun mics are great for recording ambient sound.

Lavalier Microphones

- A lavalier mic is a small, omni-directional mic that is usually attached to the subject's clothing.

- Because of their small size, lavalier mics work well for recording interviews or broadcasts.

- Lavaliers do not work well in scenes with a lot of action because the mic could fall off or rub against the actor's clothing.

- Lavalier microphones are usually battery operated and can be either wired or wireless.

RECORDING DIALOGUE

Having thought-out, well-written lines won't do any good if your audience can't hear them

Recording voices properly is a task often overlooked in low budget productions. You may have a great interview subject or actors delivering perfect lines, but none of that will matter if your audience cannot hear the dialogue.

Recorded dialogue should be as clean as possible. You should not be able to hear anything else other than the actor's voice. Avoid recording any background noise, such as traffic, birds chirping, or air conditioning. Any sound effects that are supposed to be in a scene, such as a doorbell or telephone ring, should be recorded separately and added in post-production. When your actor speaks, record his voice and only his voice.

Using a Lavalier

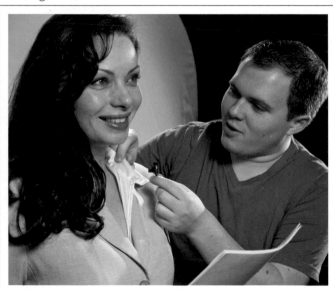

- To attach a lavalier (some-times known as a lav), first ask the subject to run the wire underneath his clothes.

- It is okay if the mic is visible, but you should never be able to see a loose wire.

- Clip the lavalier somewhere on the person's chest with the tip of the mic pointed up at the subject's mouth.

- Lavs are usually attached to the center of a shirt/blouse or to the necktie. They can also be clipped to the lapel of a suit.

Using a Shotgun Mic

- When using a shotgun mic to record an interview, get as close as possible to the subject and aim the mic directly at his face.

- If you can get your mic out of the camera frame, it is better to point the microphone down on your subject using a boom, stand, or pistol grip.

- Get as close as possible to the sound source.

- If recording outside, you may want to add a windsock or windscreen to reduce wind noise.

If you have the equipment, it is a good idea to record an actor or interview subject with the use of two different microphones. This will save you if one of your mics gets bad sound or stops working. Also, different mics have varying characteristics. By having two separate recordings, you can mix the recordings together in post-production to make the final product sound just the way you want it to.

If you only have one mic, let the person who does the majority of the speaking wear the lavalier. If everybody will speak equally, put the lavalier on the actor with the softest voice. Also, remember that an actor will always talk louder when you ask him to do a microphone check than he will when you film a scene.

Take care in evaluating the "hear-ability" of your audio. Even though you may think that you can easily hear what your actor says, the audience may not be able to. Do several tests to ensure accurate enunciation and dialogue.

Using a Boom Pole

- The most common way to record dialogue in television and film is by using a shotgun mic attached to a boom pole.

- The boom operator must place the microphone in a position that records good sound, while keeping the mic and the mic's shadow out of the shot.

- Operating a boom requires a steady hand, good arm and back muscles, and technical skill.

Using Headphones

- You should monitor the audio signal using a good pair of headphones throughout your shoot to make sure that you record quality sound.

- Bad audio is hard to fix in post-production, so it is vital that you record sound right while on set.

- If monitoring the audio while shooting is not an option, you should at the very least test it before you start filming.

RECORDING AMBIANCE
Adding ambient tones to your film creates a realistic effect on your final product

Every location that you film in will have its own distinct and subtle sounds. These environmental sounds can include animal noises, wind, running water, traffic and aircraft, machinery, human voices, or a combination of these and many other sounds. Adding these sounds to your film is the easiest way to give your film a sense of atmosphere and realism.

It is important to avoid recording under less than ideal audio conditions. Many amateur filmmakers will start filming even when there is a distracting noise in the background. This is a mistake: It is much harder to fix audio problems in post-production than to fix them on set. If you record poor-quality sound, it will always be poor-quality sound.

Room Tone

- Room tone is the sound a room has when it is silent.

- Even a room inside that seems quiet has its own ambient noise that can be later used to give the scene atmosphere.

- Either before or after you shoot an interview, you should record ambient noise that can be later used to add to the sound mix.

Ambient Sound

- Be sure to record ambient sound when filming outdoors, because you will need it during post to make your scene sound and feel more "real."

- Be sure that you are using a windscreen or windsock to cut down on any wind noise.

- You should record from different spots on the same location, so you have a variety of ambiance to choose from when mixing your sound in post.

When recording background conversation, make sure the dialogue is unintelligible so the background conversation doesn't distract listeners. When capturing street ambiance, do not record anything with a recurring sound.

Room tone is the sound of your location when there isn't any noticeable sound. You may not think it has sound to it, but it does. Record at least one minute at every location with every mic that you use. Having room tone can save you in post-production when you need to cover up unwanted sounds.

Time

- Record a minimum of thirty seconds of background ambient noise at every location that you film.

- You may think that you have enough ambient noise already, but having extra ambient sound may save you in post.

- It is important to set the levels correctly before recording, but not as important to monitor them while recording as it is with interviews.

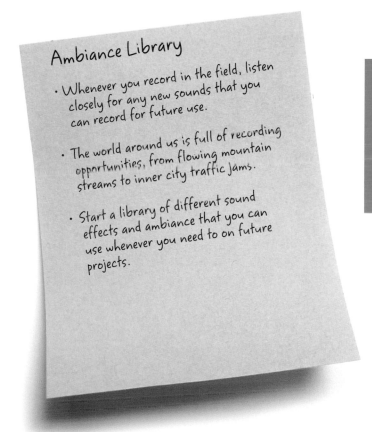

Ambiance Library

- Whenever you record in the field, listen closely for any new sounds that you can record for future use.

- The world around us is full of recording opportunities, from flowing mountain streams to inner city traffic jams.

- Start a library of different sound effects and ambiance that you can use whenever you need to on future projects.

SOUND

93

OTHER SOUND EQUIPMENT
If you are serious about audio, you'll need more than just a good mic

Having a pair of quality headphones on set is important because you will not be able to monitor sound volume and quality without them. Headphones allow you to spot bad microphone connections, dead batteries, and wireless mic interference. They help you in finding the optimal position for your shotgun mic.

In-the-ear headphones do not deliver the best sound quality, so this style headphone should not be used unless it is your only option. Over-the-ear headphones are best because they filter out all the noise coming from the outside world, allowing you to concentrate on the sound coming through the headphones.

Digital field recorders are like portable tape recorders except they record digitally and have no moving parts. They

Audio Recorders

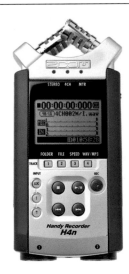

- Portable digital audio recorders can be used to capture high-quality sound while shooting without using your camcorder.

- These portable recorders typically record to SD cards or internal memory and can be connected to a com-

  puter with a USB cable for editing.

- Make sure the recorder you use can record at least CD-quality audio. It is a good idea to test the device before you use it in the field.

XLR Adapter

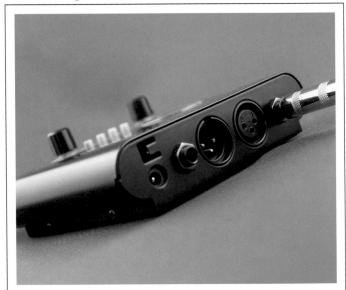

- If you want to use a professional-quality XLR microphone on your camcorder that has only a 3.5mm stereo jack, you will need an adapter.

- The XLR adapter mounts to the bottom of the cam-corder and plugs into the

  camcorder's stereo plug. It allows you to connect the more expensive XLR mics.

- XLR connections are sturdier than the 3.5mm stereo jack connections used in consumer camcorders.

can record hours of high-quality video files onto internal hard drives or memory cards. The files can then be uploaded to your computer or external hard drive and edited.

Using a digital audio recorder in conjunction with a camera that also records audio allows you to record dual system sound. The drop in price of equipment has allowed smaller productions to use this technique that was once only practiced by major Hollywood studios. Recording sound separately from two devices allows you to mix the devices in post to give you more control over the film's sound mix. Since you recorded the sound and video on two different devices, the devices will not be synced with each other, so you must sync them before editing, which can be a hassle.

Treat your sound equipment with the same care you treat all of your electronics. Avoid high temperatures, dust, dampness, and sand. Don't blow into the microphone, don't tap the head of the microphone, and don't subject the microphones to volume levels greater than they can handle.

Windsock

- Using a windscreen while filming protects your microphone and significantly reduces any wind noise you may pick up while recording outside.

- A windscreen also helps filter out a person breathing too close to the mic.

- In windy outdoor situations, you can use a windscreen, called a windsock or dead cat, which does an even better job of filtering out wind noise.

Microphone Stands/Boom Stands

- A mic stand is a good way to mount a microphone in a fixed position.

- A boom stand is the most versatile and useful type of stand and can be used in many situations.

- These mic stands are especially useful when you don't have a crew member to operate a boom pole.

- You can use clamps to mount microphones onto existing stands you may have around, such as light stands.

FINDING ACTORS
Audition a few people to find the perfect match for your film

Finding actors to star in your film can be a challenge. If you think it can be frustrating to be a filmmaker and need actors, think about what it would be like to be an actor and need filmmakers.

If you have the budget to pay actors for their work, your search for the perfect actor will go much easier. However, many actors may be willing to work for free if they like the script. Younger actors are more likely to work for free than older, more experienced ones.

People want to be involved with movies. Be enthusiastic and passionate about what you are doing and people will gather around you. Be honest when recruiting actors for your film. Make sure they know how much time they will need to block off, the shooting dates and locations, and any special

Local Theater

- Contact local theaters, high school and college drama departments, and acting schools in your area.

- Actors who work primarily on stage often are looking for a way to break into film acting.

- Stage actors are dedicated to their craft and are usually glad to work for on-camera experience, credit, and a copy of the finished project for their reels.

Online Ad

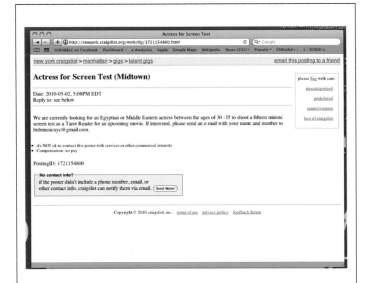

- There are many fantastic Web sites that will help your search for talented actors.

- Posting an ad on craigslist .com or mandy.com, for example, may net you hundreds of replies from interested actors.

- Some sites have actor pro-

files with detailed information on past experience, video of their work, and pay requests.

- In your ad, provide a brief synopsis of your project, what kind of actors you need, and a way for actors to get in contact with you, preferably an e-mail address.

requirements for the shoot. Part of your job as a filmmaker is to always be on the lookout for actors. There are a lot of aspiring actors out there, so chances are you know someone who knows one. And, once you find one or two actors, they will often lead you to more.

You may be able to use real people instead of trained actors for certain parts in your film. If you have a part in your film for a lifeguard, for example, find a real lifeguard to play the part. Not only will the person have experience "playing the part," but he may also be able to provide his own wardrobe.

Friends and Family

- The lure of possible fame and fortune means that many of your friends and family will be willing to give acting a try.

- This is a good option in a pinch, but you shouldn't automatically resort to casting friends and family, as it can be difficult to mix business and friends. Exhaust all other possibilities first.

- Make sure friends and family know that you are serious about your project. If they can't act or are not helping you, don't be afraid to tell them to take a hike.

Casting Director

- For bigger projects, a good casting director will have established relationships with a vast number of agents, managers, and actors that they can send to you for an audition.

- The casting director should have a good grasp of the director's needs for all of the major and minor parts in the film.

- Just like with actors, if you find a casting director that is excited about your project, he may work for free or for a reduced fee.

CASTING THE RIGHT ACTOR

Pick an actor who will be able to portray your character the way you want

Place the right actor in the right part and your production could become exactly what you hoped it would be. Cast the wrong actor and the whole thing could fall apart.

The reality is, you will not always land the perfect actor for every role in your script. Not even big budget Hollywood films cast perfectly every time. The key is to concentrate on the most important qualities that you need from an actor and be flexible on the characteristics that don't matter as much.

Before you offer a role to someone or start auditioning actors, you need to determine your talent requirements. Go through your script or outline and prepare a cast list. The list includes all major speaking roles, right down to the extras. Give a brief

Head Shot

- Before an audition, the first way to determine if an actor is a good fit for a certain role is by reviewing his head shot.

- Such scrutiny over physical appearance may seem cruel at first, but you don't have to be totally politically correct when selecting actors.

- Remember, you are casting for a specific look or part.

- If an actor doesn't have the right look for a role, you shouldn't waste your time or his time by letting him audition.

Acting Resume

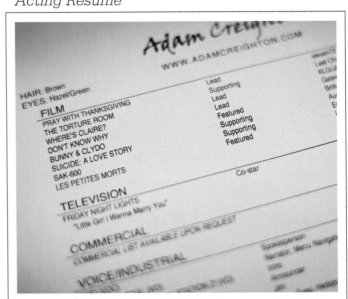

- An actor's resume will include basic things, such as his height, weight, eye color, and body type, as well as a list of all previous acting work.

- Resumes let you get a good idea of an actor's experience and the types of characters he usually plays.

- Included with the resume will be a reference list. Before you commit to any actor, you should call some past directors to see how they feel about the person's acting ability and work ethic.

description of the requirements for each role. You have to know what you're looking for before you start looking.

When working with amateur actors, you may want to typecast. Typecasting means you cast people in roles they closely resemble in look and personality. It's much easier for inexperienced actors to play characters with traits close to their own.

Look for actors with strong work ethics who are committed to you and your project. You could have the most talented actor in the world, but if he is constantly showing up late or not showing up at all, he is useless. If you lose one of the main characters in the middle of filming, it could spell disaster for the entire production. Remember, the longer your film takes to shoot, the larger the commitment required for your cast, and, ultimately, the more money out of your pocket.

Auditions

- Once you have a list of potential actors, you need to set up an audition. Give the actors a two-week lead time before the audition so they can prepare.

- It's best not to hold your auditions in your apartment or house. Find a building or location that will let you use their space for a few hours like a school gym, office building, or classroom.

- Film each actor's audition so you can compare one actor to another more easily at a later time.

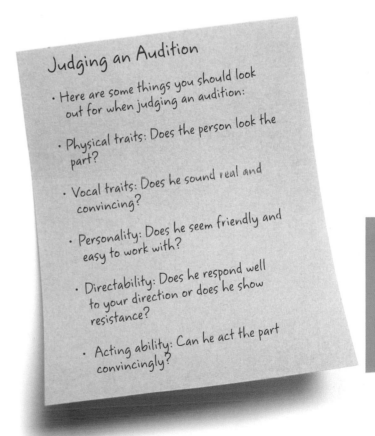

Judging an Audition

- Here are some things you should look out for when judging an audition:

- Physical traits: Does the person look the part?

- Vocal traits: Does he sound real and convincing?

- Personality: Does he seem friendly and easy to work with?

- Directability: Does he respond well to your direction or does he show resistance?

- Acting ability: Can he act the part convincingly?

THE READ-THROUGH

Going over the script with the cast benefits you as well as the actors

The read-through, or table read, is an informal get-together for the cast, crew, and director in which they sit down and read the script from beginning to end. It takes place toward the end of pre-production stage, but before you go to rehearsals. This will be the first time that you get to hear your script come to life. Doing a read-through will benefit every member involved in the project.

You need to secure a space large enough to accommodate the entire cast. A good-sized living room or garage will usually work. It is important that you get the entire cast and crew to show up for the table read. Do your best to schedule it at the most convenient time possible without conflicting with your actors' schedules. If not everyone can make it, then try your best to schedule the most important cast

The Read-through

- Actors should be provided with a copy of the script before coming to the read-through. They should have read through the script a few times by themselves to study their character.

- The process of reading through the script should be loose. Actors should read their lines with emotion, but they do not need to engage other actors or stand up and act anything out.

- Provide pens and paper for the actors so they can take notes.

Speech

- Some directors like to give a speech before the table read to explain what the story is about, while others prefer to dive right into the script so the actors are fresh and have their own perspective.

- Read from beginning to end without stopping.

- Don't allow people to ask questions or interrupt the read-through for any reason.

- Once you have read through the entire script, read it again and get the cast to talk about the scenes and raise any questions.

members first and foremost. On larger productions, this may be the last time that your entire cast is together at the same place and time.

The table read benefits everybody. It will allow everyone to be on the same page with the direction and goals you have for the movie. Hearing the entire script read through in one sitting will help the actors make choices and understand the story better when shooting a scene out of context on set. Actors often look back to the table read while on set to remember what scene comes before and what scene comes after. Having the actors on hand to read out the dialogue will give you a better sense of the story's overall flow. If you are making a comedy, you can figure out what lines are the funniest to the group at large.

Taking Notes

- As the actors read, you should take notes on lines of dialogue that don't work and sequences that could be tightened.

- Watch everyone's reactions to see if the story works. Spots where people are distracted or fidget in their seats may need work.

- As the table read continues, you may come up with additional ideas and dialogue adjustments.

- Consider filming the read-through so you can refer back to it later. You may catch things you missed the first time through.

Snacks

- Provide the cast and crew with drinks and snacks during the table read.

- You don't have to have an elaborate spread, just some coffee, bottled water, and chips, pretzels, and fruit and vegetables to munch on.

- The table read should be fun. Cast and crew members will perform better in a relaxed atmosphere.

REHEARSAL & BLOCKING

You can never have too many rehearsals, particularly with amateur actors

The last phase of pre-production is rehearsing your actors. Low budget productions often do not allow enough time for rehearsals or skip them altogether. This is a big mistake. You can never have too much time devoted to rehearsing your actors.

Rehearsing will save you time on set and allow your actors

to get comfortable with their roles before shooting begins. You don't want your actors showing up on set the first day without the proper preparation.

Before you can get to working with the actors, you've got to secure a location where you can rehearse. If you are not able to rehearse at the actual location you'll be filming, you'll need

Blocking

- Blocking is the process of determining where the actors will move and stand during a scene.

- Work with the actors during rehearsals to figure out the best position and movement within the scene. They need to know how fast to walk, where to stand, and

what lines to deliver at specific points in the camera's motion.

- Good blocking allows the actors to move naturally without making awkward crosses in front of the camera or hiding other actors in the scene.

Hitting the Mark

- Use gaffers' tape to mark places on the floor where the actors should stand at certain points during the scene.

- You need to know exactly where an actor will be in a

scene and when to properly set up your framing and focusing.

- An actor "hits the mark" when he stops at the correct spot in a scene.

to find a suitable alternative. Any large open space will do. Show the digital photos you took while scouting your location to the actors so they can get a sense of where the scene will take place.

During the first run-through, let the actors act out a scene without offering any direction. This will let the actor try different things. Actors need time to uncover and create their characters. Watch the rehearsal intently so you can offer feedback afterward.

Director's Job

- As the director you have some very important things to look for during rehearsals.

- You must unify the cast and crew and give everyone your vision for the telling of the story, including the style, rhythm, and pacing.

- It is important to develop the relationship between you and the actors, between the actors and their characters, and between each of the actors and each other.

- Try to fix any problem scenes by working with the actors or perhaps even rewriting.

"Business"

- "Business" is a film term for the actions the actor may do in a scene to make the character authentic.

- The business of a scene must be well rehearsed so it looks natural. Actors must be able to deliver their lines while doing their business and make it all appear natural.

- For example, in the scene pictured above, make sure there are enough dirty dishes in the sink and that the actress knows where the soap and sponge are located.

103

COMMUNICATION

Keep the lines of communication open with everyone on set, especially with actors

Directors and actors have a different way of looking at the script. Directors usually look at the script and the character from the outside in. The director may want the actor to perform a certain reaction, mannerism, or display a certain mood. The actor's point of view, however, comes from within. The actor will be concerned with how a character feels, what the character thinks, and what motivates the character.

These varying viewpoints can cause communication problems. If the director asks the actor to show more anger, intensity, friendliness, or enthusiasm, then the actor must interpret this from the character's point of view.

Giving specific instruction doesn't always work with actors.

Phone Numbers

- Make sure that you have phone numbers for the entire cast and crew so you can always get in contact with everyone.

- It may be a good idea to print a sheet with everybody's contact information

and give a copy to the cast and crew so they can get in contact with each other to organize rides or discuss their roles.

- Don't let anybody use his cell phone while on set. It can distract and be noisy.

One-on-one

- When you need to have a discussion with an actor, it is always better to communicate with him one-on-one instead of in a group.

- An actor may feel embarrassed if you criticize him with everybody watching.

- The actor will respond much better to advice in a one-on-one conversation because he will feel like you really care about his performance.

Telling an actor to yell, or to cry, or to be scared will cause your actor to mimic; the actor may not give a genuine performance. Instead, give the actor directions that are a means to a goal, such as: be helpful, plead, or seduce.

Good communication really is the key to getting the best performance from your actors. Let the actor know what is working and what isn't. Sometimes, just telling an actor how he appears from the outside will be enough to get him to make the necessary adjustments.

Keeping It Light

- The mood on set is also a contributing factor to performance.

- If you are filming a comedy, it is important to keep things light.

- If the scene turns to drama, a jocular mood is probably

- not appropriate, especially if the actor stays in character between takes.

- However, this doesn't mean that you have to make everybody on set sad when filming an emotional scene or angry when filming a fight scene.

Literal versus Metaphorical

- Understanding the actors' communication styles, as well as your own, will go a long way to helping you effectively communicate with each other.

- There are basically two styles of communication in conversation: literal and metaphorical.

- Literal speakers like short, detailed, to the point conversations that are used to get information across to the other person.

- Metaphorical speakers prefer longer conversations that focus on the big picture. They count on the other person to figure out the specific details of what you want and how you want it done.

ACTING

105

WORKING THROUGH PROBLEMS

How to get your production back on track when the actors are not performing

Many of the mistakes that you make on set can be fixed in post-production. Sound a little too low? Increase the volume. Video a little dark? Increase the brightness and contrast. One thing that you cannot fix in post is bad acting. The only thing you can do is cut the bad performance from the film.

Bad acting can ruin scenes and take the audience out of

a movie. One of the most challenging and important parts of directing is getting the best performance from your actor that he or she is capable of giving.

Many of these problems can be avoided by properly casting your movie. If the right actor is in the right role, your job of directing is that much easier. You can spend less time fixing

How Many Takes?

- Clint Eastwood likes to shoot his scenes in only one or two takes. This may work for Clint but it may not work for you. He has the luxury of working with the world's greatest actors while you will likely start out working with amateurs.

- Shoot as many takes of a scene as it needs to get the performance you desire from the actor.

- The more takes you shoot, the more options you have in the editing room.

Improvisation

- Encourage actors to explore improvisation and reasonable character changes.

- If your actor has trouble remembering his lines or if his delivery is flat, getting the actor to improvise can sometimes make a mediocre actor a decent one.

- Be sure you test the actor before you try this out on set, because not every actor has good improv skills.

- Even if your actor comes up with some great improvised dialogue, you still need to shoot the scene as it was written in the script.

bad performances and spend more time fine-tuning them.

A good director should have some acting background. Actors that turn into directors are able to get really good performances out of their talent because they know what the actors need. Even if you have no interest in acting and just want to direct, get some experience in plays or in front of the camera so you can better relate to your talent.

Actors Are Your Puppets

- There is nothing wrong with wanting every line said exactly as you've written it and every action done exactly as you have imagined it.

- For directors who need complete control, the actors sometimes act as puppets.

- If you are the kind of director who has a vision set in stone, make it clear to the actors from the beginning so you don't have conflict on the set.

Performance Advice

- If an actor is over-acting, and comes across as too big or animated, suggest that he lower his voice and get still.

- If the scene calls for the character to be exhausted, try shooting the scene at the end of a long, hard day.

- If the scene calls for the actor to be angry, try provoking him.

- If an actor has to cry or be sad, suggest that he recall an extremely sad moment from his life to draw upon.

- The best directors manipulate and take advantage of actors' moods and emotions to get the best performances from them.

COMPOSITION

A shot displaying good composition has interesting elements inside the frame

Composition is all about the arrangement of subject matter within the frame so the effect is as pleasing to the viewer's eye as possible. Good composition will direct the viewer's eye to the central point in your scene. Every element in your shot should have a single story to tell. Strive for shots that are aesthetically pleasing, balanced, and that show the relationship

between the different elements in the frame.

Place combinations of colors, shapes, and areas of light and dark within your shot in places that complement each other. A shot that has a lot of interesting subject matter on the right half of the frame, and nothing on the left half, would not be balanced. Balance is not the same as symmetry;

Static Shot

- The static shot is a type of shot that does not move its size, framing, or angle throughout the length of the shot, although objects in the frame can move.

- A well-composed static shot can be very effective

- because there is no camera movement to distract the viewer from what plays out in front of the camera.

- Holding a static shot for too long can become boring for the audience.

A Medium Shot

- Looking room is the space between the subject's face and the edge of the frame in the direction that he or she looks.

- There should always be more room on that side of the subject.

- When a subject moves, you should give it space within the frame to move into.

- It can be annoying to an audience to watch a subject looking off the edge of the frame or on the verge of walking out of the frame.

images don't need to be the same on each side. Just look for a secondary point of interest somewhere else in the frame to counterbalance your main focal point before you press the record button.

Scenes should be composed around a single center of interest. Each shot is a statement. If you have multiple centers of interest, viewers won't be able to easily shift their attention from one point in a frame to another. Competing centers of interest within a single frame weaken composition.

Beware of Background

- Before you start shooting, you must be very conscious of everything that is in the frame.

- If your subject stands in front of an object, such as a tree, stop sign, or building, you have to be sure that it does not appear to be growing from the subject's head.

- You may not notice this happening on location, but if not caught it will be very distracting to the audience.

Busy Background

- Keep your background as uncluttered as possible.

- A background that has too much going on can distract the audience from seeing what is important in the shot.

- It is especially important to keep your backgrounds as uncluttered as possible in digital video because your finished work will most likely be shown on a tinier screen than a movie shot on film would be.

- When in doubt, remember this acronym, K.I.S., which stands for Keep It Simple.

SHOOTING

RULE OF THIRDS

Humans react better to images when shots are composed with the Rule of Thirds in mind

Ninety percent of good composition comes from one really simple rule of thumb: the Rule of Thirds. Following this rule enables you to consistently come up with interesting, visually stimulating, well-composed shots.

Divide your frame into thirds, horizontally and vertically, and then place the interesting elements of your shot on those lines, or better yet, on the intersection of those lines. Think of it as setting a tic-tac-toe board across your viewfinder, creating nine small squares. Just like in tic-tac-toe, the center box is not always the best spot.

The Rule of Thirds is most beneficial to amateur videographers who often frame up their subjects in the dead center

Centered Composition

- When you shoot, try to avoid putting the subject in the middle of the frame.

- Centering the shot will make it appear too symmetrical and can be unappealing to the eye. The viewer's eye will not

- naturally move around to the other elements in the shot.

- Adding negative space to either side of the subject makes your shot more visually appealing.

Rule of Thirds

- The Rule of Thirds states that by dividing your shot into thirds, using two vertical and two horizontal lines, and then placing important elements of your shot on those lines or on the points where they intersect, you create a more balanced and

- more visually interesting image.

- When shooting a person, it is a good idea to line up his head with one of the vertical lines, and his eyes with the top horizontal line.

of the frame without consideration for shot composition.

Some camcorders even have the option of toggling on a guide frame overlay to help with composing shots along the Rule of Thirds lines and intersections. The Rule of Thirds is a bit easier to follow in digital photography because of the ability to crop your photos with digital editing software.

The Rule of Thirds was discovered by ancient Greek artists and has been used by almost every artist and painter since then. Look for examples of the Rule of Thirds while watching movies, looking at photographs, paintings, and sculptures.

Rule of Thirds: Landscape

- The Rule of Thirds works especially well when shooting landscapes.

- If the sky is the area of emphasis, place the horizon line along the lower horizontal line, giving the sky the top two thirds of the frame.

- Alternatively, if you want the main interest of the shot to be the land, place the horizon on the top horizontal line.

Rule (not Law) of Thirds

- Shots with good composition do not always follow the Rule of Thirds.

- You may want to center the image in your shot where you have a scene with real symmetry or a reflection.

- When your subject looks directly into the camera, a centered composition can work.

- The Rule of Thirds is just a rule, not a law. You don't have to stick to the guide religiously. Dividing your image into fourths can also work in certain situations.

SHOOTING

WIDE SHOTS
Wide shots show you a lot of information, but not much detail

It has been said that long shot ranges usually correspond to what would be the approximate distance between the front row of the audience and the stage in live theater. However, the wide shot or long shot can range in distance from very far (extreme long shot) to a shot that frames a person from head to toe. Basically, the wide shot's purpose is to allow the audience to see a large area at once. A wide shot is often used to show multiple actions taking place simultaneously, or to let the audience know where a scene takes place.

When a wide shot is used to establish a location, it is called an establishing shot. For example, assume that a scene shows a young couple enjoying a candlelit dinner. The next series of shots reveals their conversation and tells their story. But where are they? Simply adding an establishing shot could

Extreme Long Shot

- The extreme long shot is a shot where the camera is at its farthest distance from the subject.

- The main focus of an extreme long shot is to show the character's surroundings, rather than the character himself.

- Sometimes, the shot can be so long that the subject is not visible, such as a shot from space.

- For many types of films, this shot may not be appropriate.

Wide Shot/Establishing Shot

- Like the extreme long shot, the wide shot, also known as a long shot or full shot, is also used as a type of establishing shot to show the audience where they are.

- An establishing shot is used to show the audience the time and place where the scene takes place.

- When framing a person, the wide shot shows the entire human figure from head to toe.

put the couple in a cabin in the woods, a house in the suburbs, or a high rise in the city, all of which could be important to the overall scene and story.

The establishing shot is usually a locked shot, with no camera movement. A moving wide shot tends to make the audience aware of the fact that they are watching a movie, while a static wide shot sucks them into the scene.

Only use establishing shots in important scenes. If you use an establishing shot for every scene it will become too repetitive. Some filmmakers don't use establishing shots at all, preferring to get straight into the scene. Certain genres tend to use more wide shots than others. Westerns, war movies, and sci-fi movies use wide shots to show large scenery and battle scenes.

Master Shot

- The master shot is a type of wide shot that covers the entire action of a scene. It serves as the foundation on which you will add other shots and cutaways.

- The master shot is usually a locked shot, with no camera movement whatsoever.

- The master shot is still an important element of film production, but scenes are not built around the master shot in the same way that they were in the 1930s, when this technique took off.

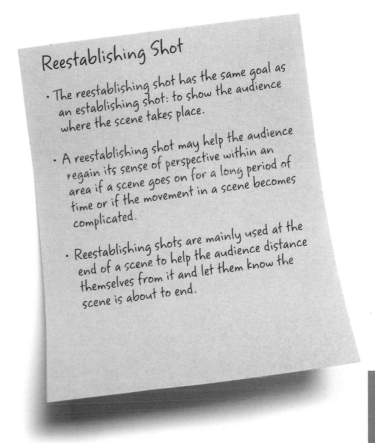

Reestablishing Shot

- The reestablishing shot has the same goal as an establishing shot: to show the audience where the scene takes place.

- A reestablishing shot may help the audience regain its sense of perspective within an area if a scene goes on for a long period of time or if the movement in a scene becomes complicated.

- Reestablishing shots are mainly used at the end of a scene to help the audience distance themselves from it and let them know the scene is about to end.

MEDIUM SHOTS
The most common type of shot used in film is the medium shot

Medium shots are generally the most common type of shots used in movies. A normal medium shot shows the character in his environment. For example, the medium shot would show a comedian on a stage. The shot would be wide enough to show the comedian and the space around him, providing a sense of context. You may not know he is a comedian, but if you see him framed in a medium shot in front of a brick wall

with a microphone in his hand, you will be able to figure it out.

It is fitting to use a medium shot when the subject speaks without too much emotion or deep concentration. The medium shot also works well when the subject delivers information, which is why television news programs frequently use it. As well as being a comfortable, emotionally

Medium Shot

- There are many variations of medium shots: waist-high shots of one person, group shots, two shots, or over-the-shoulder shots.

- Medium shots work well to show a character's body language.

- Medium shots allow you to include your character and some of your character's environment in the same shot.

Two Shot

- A two shot is a type of shot where two subjects are in the frame at once.

- Two shots are often used to establish the relationship between two people, as in the beginning of interviews.

- Two people walking and talking is a two shot. Two

- subjects side-by-side facing the camera is also a common two shot.

- A two shot of two people in profile talking to each other can be used effectively because the audience sees both characters' actions and reactions at once.

neutral shot, the medium shot allows room for hand gestures and a bit of movement.

Going directly from a wide shot to a close-up can be jarring for the audience. To get from wide to close smoothly, the medium shot is used as an effective stepping stone. Medium shots can also be used to follow characters as they move around a scene.

Using medium shots allows you a great deal of flexibility because you can eliminate the most useless parts of an image, such as a character's lower half, which typically has

little to do with the scene. When you first learn to use a camera, it is normal to want to frame everything as a medium shot because it closely resembles what you would see with your own eyes. It is important, however, to vary your shot selection; the overuse of medium shots will result in a film that resembles a soap opera.

Medium Close-up

- A medium close-up (MCU) shot usually covers the subject's head and shoulders. Two shots and over-the-shoulder shots are often medium close-ups.

- The line between medium and close-up shots can be fuzzy, but generally an MCU is halfway between

  a medium and a close-up shot.

- MCU shots show characters' facial expressions, but not as well as a close-up does.

- The medium close-up is the shot most commonly used for interviewing purposes.

Over-the-Shoulder Shot

- The over-the-shoulder shot is commonly used when two characters talk with each other and you want the audience to focus on only one character at a time.

- It is taken from behind one of the actors, using his

  back, shoulders, and head to frame one side of the shot.

- It can also be used to show what a character looks at without using a POV (point of view) shot.

CLOSE-UPS

Close-up shots are often the most dynamic and visually interesting types of shots

On a technical level, the close-up is the most difficult shot to pull off. It is challenging just to keep an actor in frame and in focus when zoomed in tight. However, the hardest part of the close-up is knowing when to use the shot.

If you use a close-up shot too early in a scene, you risk not giving the audience enough time to develop a sense of the overall scene. You may gain immediate intimacy with the actor, but lose a great deal of information conveyed through body language that may be part of the actor's performance. Use a close-up too late in a scene and you could miss showing the expressions on an actor's face during the most emotionally poignant part of the scene.

Close-ups

- A close-up (CU) shot covers the subject from the nape of the neck to just below the top of the head.

- Close-up shots of objects are often used as cutaways and inserts as a way of showing the importance of that object in the story.

- Close-up shots show the most detail of any type of shot, but do not show any of the surrounding scene.

Extreme Close-up

- The extreme close-up (ECU) is an extremely tight close-up showing only the character's eyes, nose, and mouth.

- An ECU can go even tighter focusing only on the lips, eyes, or even a single eye.

- Close-ups are also used to show small objects with a lot of detail. They suck the audience into the scene and force them to look at whatever you are focusing on.

- Extreme close-ups have grown in popularity in recent years.

The cut from the medium shot to the close-up should seem natural and should be barely noticeable to the audience. It should come at a time in the scene when it is important to know what a character feels or thinks. No better way exists for helping the audience identify with a character on screen than the close-up.

Macro Shots

- A macro lens or your camcorder's macro setting allows you to shoot an object very closely while still keeping it in focus.

- Shooting in macro mode is like looking at an object through a microscope, and allows your audience to see tiny details it wouldn't normally be able to see.

- Macro shots are often used in practical and instructional videos to show detail.

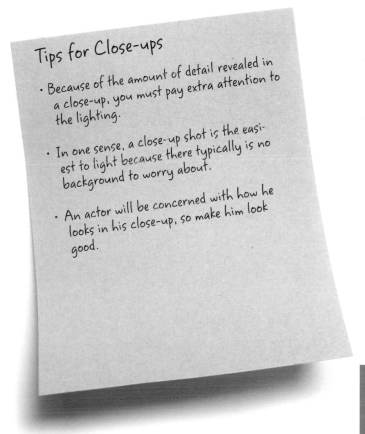

Tips for Close-ups

- Because of the amount of detail revealed in a close-up, you must pay extra attention to the lighting.

- In one sense, a close-up shot is the easiest to light because there typically is no background to worry about.

- An actor will be concerned with how he looks in his close-up, so make him look good.

SHOOTING

LINES
Your eyes follow certain lines that exist within an image

The boundaries of objects in a shot normally consist of lines: straight, curved, vertical, horizontal, and diagonal. A leading line can be almost anything: a road, path, sidewalk, fence, river, hedge, tree line, or shadow. You will not find a strong leading line around every subject, but you should look for them if they are there and take advantage of them.

Our eyes tend to travel along these lines as they move from one part of the frame to another. It becomes the job of the filmmaker to use these lines to lead the attention of the audience to the parts of the frame he wishes to emphasize. When used in this way, lines are referred to as leading lines, because they are used to lead the viewer's eyes into the frame, and generally to the scene's center of interest. Once you understand how to use leading lines, you will begin to see them

Leading Lines

- An image is often made up of multiple lines that can be any object in your frame that has a definite edge.

- A leading line is a line that leads the viewer's eyes from one part of the image to another or a line that leads the viewer to the center of interest within the frame.

- Using leading lines in conjunction with the Rule of Thirds can make for an exceptionally well-composed image.

Diagonal Lines

- Different lines within an image create different moods.

- Vertical lines are said to give the viewer a sense of strength, rigidity, power, and solidarity, while horizontal lines represent peace, tranquility, and quietness.

- Look for diagonal and curved images within your frame because the human eye is especially drawn to them.

- Strong diagonal and S-curved lines within a frame provide for a much more dynamic image.

everywhere. Leading lines don't have to be straight lines. Lines that spiral or curve can add interest and draw the view into the center of the picture. Looking down a spiral staircase or into the center of a rose are both examples of leading lines that are not straight but draw the viewer in nonetheless.

Bad Composition

- Among other things, shots with bad composition generally are shot without giving any thought to the lines in the image.

- Shots with only horizontal and vertical lines tend to be boring and lack character.

- If the image above was shot from a slightly different angle, allowing it to have diagonal lines, it would be much more interesting to the viewer.

- Lines within an image that bring your attention away from the center of interest or off the frame completely are badly composed.

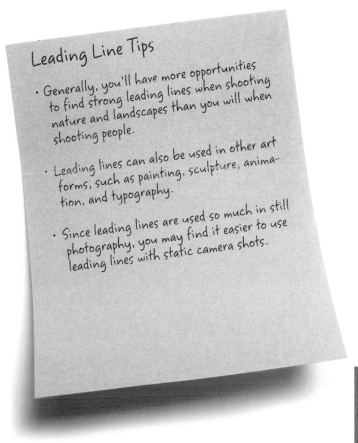

Leading Line Tips

- Generally, you'll have more opportunities to find strong leading lines when shooting nature and landscapes than you will when shooting people.

- Leading lines can also be used in other art forms, such as painting, sculpture, animation, and typography.

- Since leading lines are used so much in still photography, you may find it easier to use leading lines with static camera shots.

SHOOTING

MOVING THE CAMERA
Use the camera move that best fits the context of the scene

In the early days of filmmaking, the cameras didn't move very much. Directors believed that moving the camera would confuse people trying to follow the narrative. As moviemaking progressed, cameras started to move in all sorts of ways. Today, most productions feature a lot of camera movement, from subtle dollying along as two characters walk down a street, to elaborate crane maneuvers which fly us over a

scene and bring us in close to the action.

The key concept in camera movement is that the move must be motivated. Movement without definite purpose should not be attempted. Movement should only be used when it improves the scene. The viewer shouldn't feel like he is being moved pointlessly around the set.

There are two main motivations for a camera move. One

Hold Your Shot

- Hold your shots for at least fifteen seconds before you pan, zoom, or go on to another shot.

- That way you'll be sure to have enough video of a scene to work with later when you do your editing.

- Remember that you can always take a fifteen-second clip and make it a two-second clip during editing, but you can't take a two-second clip and make it into a fifteen-second clip.

Panning

- Don't constantly pan from side to side when you film.

- This is especially important for video that will end up on the Internet, because video with a lot of movement doesn't display well on the Web.

- Video clips need to be compressed to play on the Web; if there's lots of movement, your video will appear choppy and slow.

is to simply follow the action of the scene. If someone walks from one place to another and you don't want to do it in cuts, you need to move the camera. The other is emotional motivation, like dollying into a tighter close-up during an emotional moment, or tilting up in a close-up to make someone look more powerful.

Movement must be there for some dramatic or logical reason. When to move the camera, and why to move the camera, ultimately matter more than how you move the camera.

ZOOM

The two most basic forms of camera movement are panning and tilting; both involve the rotation of the camera while it is attached to a tripod. A pan moves the camera from side to side on a horizontal axis, providing the sense of looking to the left or the right. A tilt moves the camera up and down on a vertical axis. An even, slow speed should be maintained while panning or tilting.

Don't Zoom

- The zoom function may seem cool to somebody who hasn't used a camera before, but for the professional filmmaker or videographer, it has very little value.

- Moving the camera physically closer to what you want to film is always preferable to using the zoom.

- The only reason to use the zoom is for a shot when you can't physically get the camera where you need it to be.

- If the wind blows, or a person bumps the camera, a zoomed-in shot will show the shake more.

Shooting Action

- Anticipate action by trying to predict where the subject or action will go, and then be ready to shoot it when it moves into the frame of your shot.

- Don't be afraid to allow your subject to move out

of frame, rather than trying to follow him with your camera.

- Let action happen within the frame. Don't constantly move the camera in a useless attempt to try and catch everything.

CAMERA ANGLES

Varying the angles of shots provides interesting images and more editing options

Whether a program is fiction, documentary, music video, or any other genre, it should have style. That style is largely created through the use of varying camera angles.

In general, fiction films use moderate angles because they don't want to call attention to themselves. When edited, unobtrusive camera work allows viewers to feel they're

observing real life, rather than just watching a movie. This is especially true of comedy movies, which generally avoid the use of big close-ups and out of the ordinary camera angles.

Dramas are similar, except that they feature tighter angles to boost emotional intensity in the audience. Action pictures also use a lot of Dutch angles and elaborate camera setups.

Bird's-eye Shot

- This bird's-eye view is a shot that we are not used to seeing. Things look different and exciting and grab the viewer's attention.

- Shoot from a ladder, a balcony, a window, or even from on top of a chair. You could even mount your camera on a pole and angle

  it downward toward your subject. Cooking shows and sporting events often use shots that look straight down on the action.

- Bird's-eye view shots are often used for establishing shots or to emphasize the smallness or insignificance of a character.

Low Angle Shot

- To get the camera in a new spot nobody had tried before, Orson Welles famously chopped a hole in the floor to fit a camera and tripod at shoe level.

- Thankfully, we do not have to go through that much trouble today. All you have to do is position the

  camcorder lower than you'd normally shoot from; the lower the camcorder position, the more dramatic the effect will be.

- When viewing a scene from a low angle shot, the size and importance of the subject can be emphasized.

The trick is to save these hard-hitting setups for key moments, so they don't lose power from overuse.

Since nonfiction videos like documentaries, news features, and sports must appear to remain neutral, they typically use neutral camera angles. They favor setups that go from long shots to loose close-ups and generally avoid the use of extreme wide angle, telephoto, and off-level views.

Some cinéma vérité–style documentaries use extreme zooms, Dutch angles, and shock cuts in an effort to continually remind viewers that they are watching a movie rather than real life. Available light, lens flares, and shaky camera moves are used to enhance the feeling.

Music videos usually make no effort to hide their shooting or editing techniques. They are filled with extreme angles, editing, and camera movement.

Shooting commercials requires great care and discipline. In a message that may last as little as ten seconds, every single setup must convey a maximum amount of information in a minimum amount of time. That means finding the absolute best point of view for every shot.

POV Shot

- The point of view or POV shot gives the audience the feel that they're seeing through the eyes of the character.

- It is taken from near the eye level of the actor and shows what he might see.

- POV shots are the most common type of shots used in home videos, where the camera operator is holding the camera at eye level and walking around.

- The POV shot can also be used to show the perspective of other animals like dogs, cats, or even fish.

Dutch Angle Shot

- A Dutch angle is a type of shot that is created by simply tilting the camera so that the horizon line is angled rather than straight.

- It is often used to put viewers off balance to create a feeling of disorientation.

- If you shoot a scene with a Dutch angle, make sure you shoot a shot with a regular angle as well in case the Dutch angle doesn't work in the editing room.

- Most Dutch angles are static, although they can also be moving shots.

MOVING CAMERA SHOTS

Though hard to get just right, moving the camera creates the most impressive shots of all

Chances are a majority of your shots are at eye or shoulder level, either handheld or tripod-mounted. Adding in an unexpected angle will help break up the monotony of the video and give things a different look. It's easy to do and you really don't need anything additional in the way of equipment. All it takes is a bit of creative thinking.

Be prepared to experiment. Think about some of the things you'd like to try doing, then try them at a time that doesn't matter. Experimenting is half the fun of making videos, and coming up with a new move that wows viewers while helping to get your story across is extremely satisfying. Most new techniques take practice and experimentation to achieve

Dolly Shot

- A dolly is a shot that has motion toward or motion from a subject.

- The name comes from the old dolly tracks that used to be laid down for the heavy camera to move along before Steadicams got so popular.

- The phrase "dolly-in" means step toward the subject with the camera, while "dolly-out" means to step backward with the camera, keeping the zoom the same.

Trucking Shot

- Trucking is like dollying, but it involves motion left or right.

- Truck left means moving the camera physically to the left while maintaining its perpendicular relationship.

- The truck shot should not be confused with a pan, where the camera remains firmly on its axis while the lens turns to one direction or the other.

- You might truck to stay with a person as he walks down a street.

success, and good camera work requires experience.

The best way to get professional-looking camera moves is to treat your video camera as if it is thirty pounds heavier. Typically, that means slowing movement down, using a tripod, and keeping shots as steady as possible with whatever bracing is available.

If you're going to pan and/or tilt, make sure that you'll be comfortably positioned throughout the whole move. You don't want to start a pan and then realize you can't reach around far enough to get the end of it. If it's going to be difficult, you're better off finding the position that is most comfortable at the end of the move, so that you start in the more awkward position and become more comfortable as you complete the move.

If you want nice reverse dolly shots, you should learn to walk backward. Have someone place his hand in the middle of your back and guide you. If done smoothly, these shots can look great.

Pedestal Shot

- Performing a pedestal shot involves moving the camera up or down without changing its vertical or horizontal axis.

- There are only two types of pedestal shots: Pedestal up means move the camera up while pedestal down means move the camera down.

- Visualize your camera on a tripod and act as if you are raising or lowering the tripod head. You are not tilting the lens up; rather you are moving the entire camera up.

Handheld Shot

- When the action moves too quickly or too unpredictably, the camera may have to come off the tripod.

- The camera will simply be held by the operator, who will then perform a number of basic camera moves by moving his feet and torso: trucking in and out, dollying in one direction or another, tilting, panning, zooming, etc.

- The handheld shot is perceptibly shakier than that of a tripod-mounted camera shot.

180-DEGREE RULE

This rule should always be in the back of your mind when shooting a scene

Crossing the line is a very important concept in video and film production. It refers to an imaginary line that cuts through the middle of the scene, from side to side with respect to the camera. Crossing the line changes the viewer's perspective in such a way that it causes disorientation and confusion. For this reason, crossing the line is something to be avoided.

All coverage shots in a scene should be shot from one side or the other of this imaginary line. The audience subconsciously forms a mental map of where the actors are located in the scene and from the first master shot will be thinking that "Rosa is on the left and Chris is on the right."

If you go to a close-up of Rosa filmed from the other side

Crossing the Line

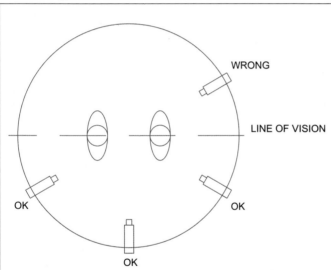

Breaking the Line

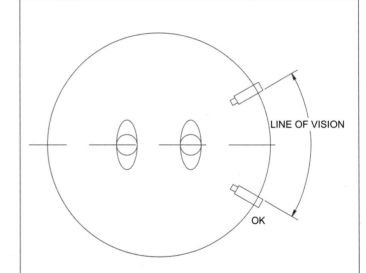

- Each scene has an axis of action drawn across the frame or screen. In most scenes, the axis is formed by drawing a line between the two characters.

- The 180-degree rule is a basic guideline in filmmaking. Two characters or other elements in the same scene should always have the same left-right relationship to each other.

- If the camera passes over the imaginary axis connecting the two subjects, it is called crossing the line.

- To break the 180-degree rule, you must move the camera across the line while shooting.

- A Steadicam operator tracking around the subjects while shooting is a continuous flow of action and does not break the 180-degree rule.

- You can also shoot a direction neutral shot where the actor looks directly into the camera or, in the case of a car chase, the car comes right at the camera, and then cut to any other shot without breaking the 180-degree rule.

of the line, it will suddenly appear that Rosa has jumped to the right side of the set. This kind of change is very confusing to viewers and briefly takes them out of the story as they attempt to reestablish their understanding of where everyone is located. You want to avoid anything that takes your audience out of the emotion of the scene.

In the case of one actor walking down the street, if the first shot shows him walking from the left to the right, then all other shots should show him walking from the left to the right. If you jump to the other side of the line it will look like

the character has suddenly decided to return to where he came from.

The difficulty comes when you have a circle of actors in a room or seated around a table. The line will change position as the dynamics of the conversation change.

Violating the Rule

- Imagine we are watching a football game. Team A is on the left side of the screen trying to score on the right side of the screen. Switching to a shot where Team A is rushing into the end zone on the left side of the screen would be crossing the line.

- We, the viewers, may get confused and think that Team A just scored on its own end zone.

- Moral of this lesson? If you decide to shoot a football game from the home side of the field, make sure all of your cameras are on that side.

Breaking the 180-degree Rule

- Rules are made to be broken, but you must understand the screen dynamics of breaking the 180-degree rule before crossing the line.

- Sometimes the rule is broken intentionally because the filmmakers want the audience confused in a moment of intense action or physical distress.

- The rule can also be broken without confusing the audience by cutting to wide shots on the other side of the line, so the audience is well aware of how the characters are placed within the scene.

SHOOTING INTERVIEWS

Interviews are a staple of documentary film, reality TV, and news programs

The interview is a fundamental element of video and television production, used in a wide range of programming. Interviews are a very efficient way of creating content. They are cheap to produce, effective for gathering and presenting information, and easy to edit. Entire programs can be made using little more than interviews laced with cutaways.

The better prepared you are, the better your interview will turn out. Set the interview in an appropriate location, perhaps with relevant background features. Sit-down interviews are conventionally conducted in the world of the subject. They are done in people's homes, their place of work, or wherever they live their lives. Interview locations should say

Interviewer Included

- One way of setting up an interview is including the interviewer in the shot.

- The Oprah Winfrey Show and The Tonight Show use this style of interview setup. It is often used when you

- have a celebrity or professional journalist as the interviewer.

- Use this technique when the audience is interested in the question and the questioner as well.

Most Common Interview Style

- In most cases, the interview subject faces slightly left or right of the camera.

- This shows that the subject is talking to someone besides the viewer, but by being relatively front-on, the viewer is still part of the conversation.

- Normal people being interviewed are much more relaxed, much more honest, when they have a human face to look at and talk to.

- People like seeing someone's whole face when they talk. Avoid severe profile shots.

something about the character. If you're outside you could use an identifiable building or landmark; if you're inside you could use photos, logos, etc.

In addition to the interview itself, it is important to get other shots. B-roll is video that you can cut together over the interviewee's voice. Usually the footage relates to the subject being discussed by the interviewee. For example, if the interviewee is discussing his band, then you would want to get some shots of the band performing, and other related shots.

Reality TV Style

Close-up Interview Style

- Some interviews have the interview subject looking directly into the camera.

- Looking into the lens has become common for confessional-type interviews, like the talking head interviews in reality television and personal documentaries.

- It can be intimidating to the viewer to see someone looking straight at them, because it brings the viewer closer to the person.

- Use this style when the video is instructional, or when the interview subject is commentating.

- Interviews tend to use shots ranging from wide shots to medium to close-ups.

- In evening news, everyone is framed in a medium shot with the occasional wide angle showing the entire news desk with all the anchors and any guests on the show. This is because

- the emotional condition of your local news anchor isn't important.

- Shots tighter than a MCU are appropriate for when the guest is talking about something personal or emotional. The shot pulls the viewer into the same emotional space.

DEPTH OF FIELD

Experiment with the focus and depth of field to come up with exciting shots

The depth of field in an image is the portion of the image that appears to be sharp and in focus. The creative use of focus depends on being able to control what is and is not in focus. Know what you want to be sharp and what you want to be soft. You can direct your viewer's attention by making the main subject the sharpest part of the frame, no matter where in the frame that subject appears.

If you want the viewer to see everything in your image and give each object equal importance, the entire image should be in focus and therefore you should use a wide depth of field. If there is a single object, person, or group that take priority over all else in the image, using a narrower depth of

Rack Focus

Deep DOF

- A rack focus is when the filmmaker changes focus within a single shot in order to draw the viewer's attention to something else.

- There are two objects on screen: one close to the camera, and one farther off in the distance, but still visible. The camera will be focused on one of the objects, and then will shift focus to the other object.

- With digital camcorders, rack focus should be done with your camera on a tripod and in manual focus mode.

- Most consumer-level camcorders have very deep depths of field in most shooting situations.

- Decrease the distance between the camera and your subject and more of your shot will be in focus.

- 35mm film has a significantly larger imaging surface than most DV or HDV cameras, which usually have ¼- to ⅓-inch CCDs. This causes video cameras to have a much deeper depth of field than film.

field will help to draw the viewer's eye to them.

In order to shoot with a wide depth of field, your camera's lens needs to be set at a wide angle. You can achieve this by simply zooming all the way out. Shots where you have multiple objects, whose distances from the camera vary greatly, such as landscapes and horizons, are best captured with a wide depth of field.

If you want to focus in on a particular subject, your image will look more natural if you use a narrow field depth. To narrow your depth of field, move away from your subject, and then zoom in. Of course, the camera should be locked down on a tripod before zooming in.

After you have set up a shot with a narrow depth of field, it's important to make sure your subject stays in focus. Movement toward or away from the camera could put the subject out of focus quickly, depending on just how narrow your field depth is.

Shallow DOF

- Getting shallow depth of field out of a digital video camcorder takes a little effort, and a larger area to shoot in.

- Make sure your camera's iris is open all the way. A wide-open iris will give you the shallowest depth of field.

- You need your foreground subject well away from the background and the camera far from the subject.

- To accentuate the shallow depth of field effect, zoom in as much as possible.

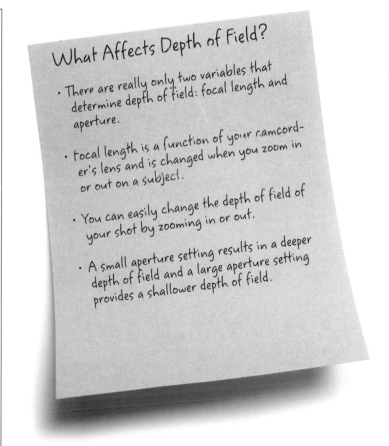

What Affects Depth of Field?

- There are really only two variables that determine depth of field: focal length and aperture.

- focal length is a function of your camcorder's lens and is changed when you zoom in or out on a subject.

- You can easily change the depth of field of your shot by zooming in or out.

- A small aperture setting results in a deeper depth of field and a large aperture setting provides a shallower depth of field.

EDITING HISTORY
The editing room is where you build your story

The very first films were simple shots of an event taking place, such as a ship pulling into a harbor, a horse galloping, or a train passing by. These films didn't have a story and didn't contain any editing.

Shortly after this, French filmmakers the Lumiere Brothers, and the Edison Company, started producing films that contained a plot and a story, but these films still did not contain

much editing. Since filmmaking evolved from the theater, it was thought that scenes should be captured in one take. The early filmmakers thought that splicing together different shots from various angles would confuse the audience. The only editing that took place was the splicing of scenes together to make the films longer.

Eventually, early filmmakers such as Edwin S. Porter and

Flatbed Editing

- The Moviola was an upright editing machine that was the standard film editing system throughout much of Hollywood's history, until the 1970s.

- The German-made Steenbeck, or KEM, surpassed the Moviola in speed and

  sound quality, and it operated more quietly, with larger viewing monitors.

- These flatbed editing systems were used until they were eventually replaced by nonlinear editing systems in the 1990s.

Women Editors

- Many women were employed as editors in the early twentieth century because editing was not considered creative work, but rather a detailed technical job similar to sewing.

- This allowed many young women to break into the industry and leave their mark on early Silent Era films.

- Successful women editors throughout the history of film include Thelma Schoonmaker (Martin Scorsese's editor since Raging Bull), Dede Allen (Bonnie & Clyde, Reds, Dog Day Afternoon), and Sally Menke (editor of all of Quentin Tarantino's films).

D. W. Griffith discovered that cutting, or editing, strips of films did not destroy the viewer's ability to comprehend the flow of images. Rather, they realized that by editing shots into a sequence they could tell more complex stories. Editing evolved quickly after that discovery. By 1916, D. W. Griffith was making sophisticated films with changing shot sizes and camera positions.

ZOOM

Edwin S. Porter introduced the technique of dramatic editing. In 1902, Porter made the breakthrough film *Life of an American Fireman*, which was among the first films that had a plot, action, and close-ups. Porter's *The Great Train Robbery* was one of the first examples of dynamic, action editing. He pieced together scenes shot at different times and places to create an emotional impact.

Film Splicer

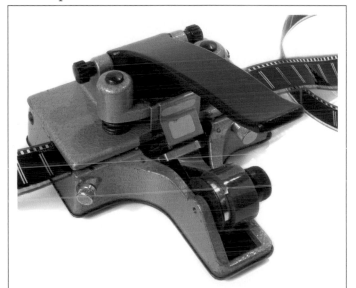

- A film splicer (known as a film joiner in Europe) is a device that is used to physically join together lengths of film.

- Traditionally, film was edited by cutting sections of the film to rearrange together or discard.

- The process of splicing is very straightforward. The splicing machine allows film footage to be lined up and held in place while it is cut, or spliced, together.

Linear Editing System

- Linear editing was the original method of editing electronic videotapes before editing computers became available in the 1990s.

- This method of editing is called "linear" because the editing has to be done from beginning to end, in a linear fashion.

- If the editor changed her mind or noticed a mistake, it was almost impossible to go back and re-edit an earlier part of the video.

- This kind of editing required at least two VCRs connected together. One acted as the source, the other as the recorder.

GOALS OF EDITING

The primary goal of editing is to construct your shots into a cohesive story

Editing is arguably the most important element of film or video production. Movies are made in the editing room, and film and video editing is an art form. It is in the editing, the art of arranging pictures, dialogue, and sounds, where your project truly comes to life. Days, weeks, even months of shots captured on video must be studied, interpreted, analyzed, and finally arranged in the most effective way possible to communicate your story.

When we watch a movie, we don't focus on the thousands of separate images that make up the movie, but instead we get lost in the story, taking for granted the multiple camera positions that give us views that we would never be able to

Deleting Footage

- Removing unwanted footage is the simplest and most common task in editing.

- Videos—especially the pacing of your story—can be dramatically improved by simply getting rid of the flawed or unwanted parts.

- Editing allows you to trim down your videos to make them more exciting. A three-hour baseball game can be compressed into two minutes of exciting highlights, which is much more manageable for the sometimes impatient audience.

Separating by Takes

Name	Duration	In	Out	Media Start	Media End	Tracks	Good
▼ ☐ Scene 3							
▶ ☐ A							
▶ ☐ B							
▼ ☐ C							
🎬 Scene 3 – Locked	00:00:00;00	Not Set	Not Set	01:00:00;00	01:00:00;00	1V, 4A	
▼ ☐ Scene 4							
▼ ☐ A							
▼ ☐ A-Camera							
🎬 4A–Acam–Take1.MOV	00:00:05:10	Not Set	Not Set	00:00:00;00	00:00:05;09	1V, 2A	
🎬 4A–Acam–Take2.MOV	00:01:21:02	Not Set	Not Set	00:00:00;00	00:01:21:01	1V, 2A	
🎬 4A–Acam–Take3.MOV	00:00:14:01	Not Set	Not Set	00:00:00;00	00:00:14:00	1V, 2A	
▶ ☐ B-Camera							
▶ ☐ B							
🎬 Scene 4	00:00:00;00	Not Set	Not Set	01:00:00;00	01:00:00;00	1V, 4A	
▼ ☐ Scene 5							
▼ ☐ A							
▶ ☐ B							
▶ ☐ C							
🎬 Scene 5 – Rough	00:00:00;00	Not Set	Not Set	01:00:00;00	01:00:00;00	1V, 4A	
▶ ☐ Scene 6							

- With digital video, it is common to shoot far more footage than you will actually need to tell your story.

- You will likely have multiple takes with multiple angles of the same scene. This is great because it gives you the creative freedom you need in the editing room.

- The editing room is where you decide which shots work best for the story.

- The actor's performance should be the most important factor when deciding between one take and another.

experience in our own lives. The editing process occurs in three basic steps: capturing, editing, and putting the product in a distributable form. During the capture phase, the actual shots are compiled into a format from which they can be edited on your computer. During the editing process, the collection of shots is organized in a desired sequence and sound is added through sound mixing until all parts form a comprehensive storyline. Once this has been accomplished, the film or video is finalized in the desired format, whether it be a DVD for distribution or a video file for online sharing.

Adding Music and Graphics

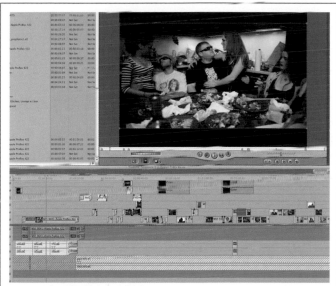

- Today's editing programs make it easy to add music, pictures, special effects, and many other elements to your videos.

- Most videos can be improved by adding extra elements.

- When editing, experiment with different music tracks, special effects, and graphics. You'll be surprised how much you can change the feel of a video by adding these extra elements.

······· YELLOW ● LIGHT ·······

Unedited, raw video footage can be painful to watch. It's usually choppy and jumpy, with scenes stretching out way too long. By removing the bad bits of the video and keeping the good parts, the timeline of your story gets smoothed out and pacing improves tremendously. Your video becomes much more watchable and enjoyable for the audience.

Criteria for a Cut

- Walter Murch is a film editor and author of a book on film editing titled *In the Blink of an Eye*. Murch states that there are certain criteria that should be at the top of an editor's list while working.

- A cut must reflect what an audience is meant to feel.

- A cut must advance the story.

- Editing should make the shots flow together rhythmically.

CONTINUITY EDITING

Editing to preserve a story's consistency is the predominant style for television and feature films

Continuity editing is the dominant style of editing used in narrative films. Nearly all Hollywood films are put together following the rules of continuity. Films are cut in a way so that each shot should complement its predecessor and so that the viewer easily comprehends what happens.

As an editor, you will likely have hundreds of scenes and takes of scenes available to you to use to construct your story. The shots you select to build a scene should logically trace a series of events to their conclusion. Anything—be it a scene or a portion of a scene—that appears to put things out of order or breaks the natural flow of a story is said to break continuity. The editing should be seamless so that the audience

Cutting on Action 1

Cutting on Action 2

- Cutting on action is a standard editing technique that creates a smooth cut from one shot to another.

- The edit brings together two shots of the same action from different angles or shot sizes.

- The two shots may have been shot hours apart, but the cut gives the impression of continuous time.

- When done well, the cut will not be noticed by the audience.

- The cut must be placed at the correct moment so the energy and motion from the first shot carries smoothly into the next shot.

- In the image sequence above, the first shot ends

- with the actress turning her head to look behind her.

- We cut to the next shot half way to three quarters through the actress's head turn to create a seamless cut.

stays focused on the story instead of the techniques used.

The establishing shot, breakdown, and reestablishing shot represent the classic shot sequence used for scenes in continuity editing. This sequence begins with a wide establishing shot to give an overall sense of the location and physical position of the characters within that location. The breakdown is the series of medium shots and close-ups that provide the energy and focus of the scene. And the reestablishing shot is another wide shot to reestablish the location and relationships of the characters.

Many art house films purposely break continuity to challenge the conventions of Hollywood. This breakdown of continuity tries to make the audience aware of the fact that they are watching a movie, something Hollywood films try to avoid. This is done through the use of jump cuts, non-diegetic inserts, and by challenging the logical progressions of plots and subplots.

EDITING

Eye Line Matches

- Eye line matches show the relationships between characters and objects in a scene.

- When viewers see a character looking off screen followed by another shot, they think the person from the first shot is looking at the object in the second shot.

- The theory is that the audience will want to see what the character on screen is looking at, so you should show them.

- Any interaction between characters usually requires an eye line match in order to maintain continuity between edits.

Cross Cutting

- Cross cutting is an editing technique used to show simultaneous action happening at two different locations.

- Cross cutting is often used in chase scenes. One shot will show a character running or hiding, and then the film will crosscut to another character giving chase or searching around.

- The frequency and length of the crosscuts play a large part in determining the tension and suspense of a scene.

137

TRANSITIONS
Transitions pull the story from one shot to the next

The way in which any two shots are joined together is called a transition. It is important to understand the different transitions and when they should be used.

Each transition sends the audience a unique subconscious message about what happens in your film. The audience will follow your film more easily when the transitions support what happens in the story.

In the classical continuity style, editing techniques should avoid drawing attention to themselves. This is why the cut is by far the most commonly used transition. It is simple and effective. Used properly, cuts could be the only transition you'll ever need. Avoid the temptation to use some of the fancy transitions that come with your editing software. Keep your transitions as smooth and as unnoticed as possible.

Straight Cut

- The cut is the most common type of transition. It is an instant change from one shot to another.

- Cuts are the best way to keep the action or momentum moving along at a good pace.

- Straight cuts are not only simple, but they create smaller overall file sizes, which are an advantage for Web videos.

Dissolves or Cross Fades

- The dissolve is a gradual fade from one shot to the next. It is also known as a cross fade.

- Dissolves are usually used to convey a sense of passing time or a change in location.

- Since the dissolve has been used so much throughout the history of film to show a change in time or place, using it for any other reason may confuse the well-trained audience.

In the rare case where a simple cut, dissolve, or fade just won't work and you must use another type of transition, there are a few things you must keep in mind. You must be consistent with the use of transitions. For example, if you use a circular wipe when changing locations, be consistent in using a circular wipe. Mixing and matching a bunch of different styled wipes will look amateurish and will confuse the audience. Transitions should also be kept short, between .5 and 1.5 seconds.

Many films start with a short fade from black. Early filmmakers adapted this technique from theater to emulate the look of the stage lights coming on at the beginning of a play. A more dramatic opening would be a cut from a black background. Cutting straight from black pulls viewers into your story quickly because it makes them feel as if they missed something and need to catch up.

Wipe Transition

- The wipe transition is a gradual transition from one image to another where one shot is replaced by another with a distinct edge. The edge of the wipe may be hard or soft.

- There are many different types to use, including the iris wipe, star wipe, heart wipe, or any other shape you can think of. Using a wipe is a stylistic choice that tends to makes the audience more aware that they are watching a film.

Digital Transitions

- All editing programs offer a wide variety of digital transitions with various effects.

- Some of these effects include color replacement, checkerboards, and pixilation.

- Most camcorders also include digital transition features and effects such as fades and wipes.

- If you use the transitions found on your camcorder, you will be stuck with those transitions on your footage forever; it is always better to add these effects in post-production instead.

PACING
Your film has to have perfect flow to it: not too slow, not too fast

Pacing is the most important aspect of film editing. It contributes to the film's mood and overall impression on the viewer. It is also one of the most complex things to analyze, since pacing is achieved through the combination of production design, cinematography, sound, and editing.

Rhythm, which is part of the overall pacing, can be understood as the final balance of all of the elements of a film. The rhythm of a scene is mostly affected by how you choose to edit together the shots. Using long, slow pans and static shots results in a slow pace while cutting together quick close-ups and action shots makes for a faster pace.

If the pace of your video is too slow, you can add more cuts or more video clips. If your pace is too fast, it can tire out an audience and make the information hard to grasp. The best

Bored Audience

- Beginning editors tend to make sequences way too long, which will bore the audience.

- When cutting between two shots of a person crossing a room, for example, you do not need to show every step the character takes.

- Viewers can take in a lot of information in just a few seconds.

- After you cut your scene, walk away from it and come back later. The pacing will likely feel too slow and you may want to cut it even more.

Close-up

- One effective way to increase the pace of your video and to make it more visually appealing is to insert close-up shots.

- For example, if your character walks toward a car to leave, you can insert a close-up of him inserting the key into the door to unlock it.

- Add a close-up of your hero unholstering his gun before a gunfight, or a close-up of a man slipping a ring onto his girlfriend's finger.

way to slow down the pace is to eliminate some clips and stay with the shots longer. The ability to alter the pace of a scene greatly depends on the variety of coverage you shot. The more source video—video you shot while on set—you have access to, the easier it will be to edit together a scene.

Different Pacing

- Determining the pace of your video is largely dependent on your target audience.

- Generally, the younger the audience, the faster the pace they can comfortably tolerate.

- People in today's world of Twitter and text messages are used to consuming information fast; what was considered normal pacing twenty years ago is likely considered slow today.

What's the Correct Pace?

- Determining the right pace for your video can be one of the hardest parts of video editing.

- Once your scene is cut, take a break and come back to it later. With fresh eyes you will be able to tell if the story flows well.

- Nonlinear editing offers you the advantage of using trial and error. You can make cuts, and if they don't work, you can easily adjust them until they do.

MONTAGE

Montage uses short shots edited into a sequence to condense space, time, and information

Montage is a type of editing style that is used in video and film production. A montage gets its power from presenting a collection of diverse images to the audience all at once, so that the overall impression is much richer than simply showing a single image or shot.

The term "montage" has different meanings in French,

American, and Soviet cinema. In French cinema, montage (translated to "putting together" or "assembly") simply refers to editing. American montage is usually used to show the passage of time, such as the training montage in the movie *Rocky*. When most people think of montage, they think of this style.

Soviet montage is something different altogether. Soviet

Jump Cut

- A jump cut is a cut in film editing in which two sequential shots of the same subject are taken from camera positions that vary only slightly.

- This type of edit causes the subject of the shots to

  appear to jump position. Jump cuts are considered a violation of classical continuity editing.

- A jump cut can also be made by removing the middle section of a video clip.

Frame-by-frame

- Precise editing is done on the frame-by-frame level.

- Your editing software will allow you to zoom in to the timeline so that you can see individual frames of your video.

- It may not seem like cutting off a frame that is only 1/30 of a second long will make a difference, but it may be enough editing to make a shot that doesn't work, work.

montage is a type of cinema that relies heavily upon editing and attempts to convey meaning to the viewer based on the context of different shots. Early Soviet filmmakers disagreed on exactly how to view montage.

The father of montage, Sergei Eisenstein, believed that film montage could have an impact beyond the individual images. He believed that editing together two or more images created something else entirely, that made the whole greater than the sum of its parts. His most famous example of this is the Odessa steps sequence in *The Battleship Potemkin*.

Time Code

TC1 01;33;27;29;

- Time code is an eight-digit code used in editing that allows you to specify precise video and audio points.

- Using time code allows you to cut more precisely and saves time. For example, editing instructions like, "cut the scene when the door slams shut," leave room for interpretation. Cutting on "00:00:01:08" refers to one very specific point.

- The string of numbers in a time code may seem imposing, but their meaning is simple: 1 hour, 33 minutes, 27 seconds and 29 frames is equivalent to 01:33:27:29.

Match Cut

- A match cut is two shots of the same action from different angles.

- Match cuts ensure that the action in a scene is not interrupted in any way.

- A good match cut is often not noticed by the audience.

- A match cut may also be a type of edit where the two camera shots' compositional elements match. For example, in the edit in *2001: A Space Odyssey*, a bone thrown by an ape is matched with a flying spacecraft.

NONLINEAR EDITING
With computers you can access any frame in a video with ease

What most people mean by NLE or nonlinear editing actually has nothing to do with editing. This term simply refers to working with digitized film and video media.

Nonlinear editing for films and television in post-production is a modern editing method that allows one to access any frame in a digital video clip with the same ease as any other. The video files on your hard drive are just like normal Word documents: you can load, watch, and manipulate any part of the file in a nonlinear mode. You can then edit and rearrange the shots much like moving paragraphs around in your word processing program. Since the video is digitized, you instantly can get to any exact point in the video.

Once you have stored the video on your PC, you can arrange clips on a timeline using your video editing software. You can

Home Editing System

- Many old computers won't support video editing, and many new computers will only work with the most basic editing software.

- Your computer has to be fast, with sufficient memory and with the latest graphics

and audio cards, to support real-time media work.

- For the editing software to work perfectly, you should at least double the computer specifications the software manufacturer provides.

RAM

- If your computer only slows down slightly when you edit video, it may be that you just need to add more memory (RAM).

- Your computer should have at least 2 gigabytes of RAM for optimal performance.

- If your computer has open slots for RAM, you can add another gigabyte or two to speed it up.

- The more money you spend, the better performance you will get.

lay down more than one track of video and audio onto the timeline. When you rearrange and edit your video clips, the original footage is never altered. The timeline merely points to "in" and "out" points in the clips on your hard drive, so any changes you make can be easily undone.

ZOOM

Today, nonlinear editing is king and linear editing is considered obsolete. Still, you should have some idea of how it worked. In the early days of video production, linear editing was the only way to edit videotapes. This mechanical process involved camcorders, VCRs, edit controllers, Titlers, and mixers to perform the edit functions. Editing was performed in linear steps, one cut at a time.

Dual Monitor

- In a video editing environment, dual displays can be very useful.

- Some applications are designed for dual displays and will give you a highly optimized workspace.

- Not all applications will stretch across the second screen, but you can still use that second screen for locating your media files, checking your e-mail, etc.

- Once you edit on a dual-screen display, it will be hard to go back to a single monitor.

Editing Keyboards

- Editing keyboards have color-coded keys that are named and marked with icons that indicate their functions. These key commands allow editors to perform many functions quickly without needing to navigate through software screens using the mouse.

- If you don't want to buy a new keyboard, you can buy stickers that go over your existing keys.

- If you spend a lot of time doing advanced editing, a keyboard can be helpful, but it is not necessary for the average filmmaker.

CAPTURING

How do you get the video you shot onto the computer and ready for editing?

Once you record your footage, you need to get it onto your computer so you can edit it. This process is called capturing video footage and is simply the means by which you transfer the footage to a place where you can alter it from its original format, length, sequential order, and/or quality.

Hard disk cameras are the easiest piece of equipment to capture from, because instead of having to play your tape or DVD back and record that footage as a digital video file in real time, you can simply drag and drop the files from the camera's hard drive to your workstation. It's essentially the same thing as getting photos off of a digital camera.

Once you're connected to your editing system, you can pull

The USB Port

FireWire Port

- The way you capture your footage onto your computer varies depending on the camcorder you use. Many camcorders use USB.

- As of fall 2006, USB 2.0 remains the current standard and is theoretically capable of transfer speeds up to 480 megabits per second.

- USB 3.0 promises a major leap forward in transfer speeds and capability, while maintaining backwards compatibility with USB 2.0 devices.

- USB 3.0 will be able to transfer data ten times faster than USB 2.0.

- Almost all recently manufactured camcorders have a FireWire port (also called IEEE 1394 or iLINK).

- Due to the extremely fast transfer speeds that FireWire achieves, digital video will transfer with almost zero loss in quality.

- Not all computers come with FireWire ports. If your computer has no FireWire port, you can buy an expansion card.

up a folder view of all the files available and grab whichever ones you want.

With MiniDV tape, you'll need to connect your camera to your computer workstation and choose the segments you want to use. You could watch the tape and assemble a detailed shot list, complete with time code locations for each shot, or load the entire tape at once.

If most of your footage is at least usable and your computer storage capacity is adequate, you may prefer to simply capture an entire tape or disc at once.

External Hard Drive

- HD digital video footage takes up a lot of drive space, and you'll need somewhere to put it. External hard drives offer additional storage space.

- Before you buy a hard drive, consider how much hard drive storage space you need and keep in mind how much you will need in the future.

- If your computer has a lot of internal hard drive space, you may be able to put off buying an external hard drive for a while, but you will eventually need one.

•••••••••••• RED ● LIGHT ••••••••••••

When you edit a video, it isn't actually imported into your project file. The project simply references the copy of the video wherever it is stored on your hard drive. This means that if you move the file, delete it, change the filename, or change any folder name along the file path, your editing software isn't going to find it.

Mac versus PC

- The Mac versus PC debate has been raging for years: Which platform is better for video editing?

- Some people swear by Apple's Macintosh platform while others insist on working only within the Windows universe.

- PCs generally offer better value, a wider choice of components, and easier upgrade paths.

- One advantage to using a Mac is that you can use Final Cut Pro, one of the most popular editing programs.

- Ultimately, the choice comes down to personal preference.

EDITING II

147

EDITING PROGRAMS

Information on some basic editing programs that anyone can easily edit video with

Editing software comes in all flavors, from free online editing software you can use anywhere to editing software that costs thousands and requires a powerful computer. Which editing software is right for you?

Before you buy any video editing software, give the free stuff a try; you may find that it works for your project. iMovie (Macs) or Movie Maker (PCs) comes installed on new computers. If you don't already have one of these video editing programs, you can easily get it cheaply or for free. The features, graphics, and special effects are often perfect for hobby video enthusiasts as well as beginning video editors looking to experiment.

iMovie

- iMovie is a simple, easy-to-use video editing program that comes free with the Apple operating system.

- iMovie HD includes support for HDV and integration with the rest of the iLife suite.

- iMovie offers many of the same features, such as dropping clips on a timeline, cropping them, and adding transitions between clips, as more advanced video editing programs like Final Cut Pro.

Movie Maker

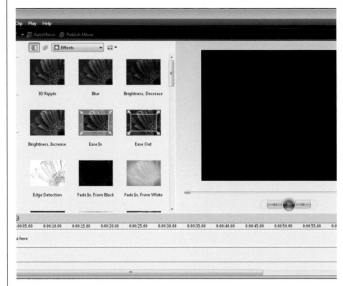

- Windows Movie Maker comes standard on newer versions of the Windows operating system.

- This program is very small and does not have many system requirements to run. The software is designed to run on any standard home computer.

- It contains features such as effects, transitions, titles/credits, audio track, timeline narration, and auto movie.

- Windows Movie Maker is also a basic audio track editing program. Audio tracks can be exported in the form of a sound file instead of a video file.

The Internet is filled with downloads that let you upgrade iMovie and Movie Maker by adding advanced audio, visual, and graphic effects. Use these add-ons to customize your video editing system based on the features you need.

Video editing software that is more sophisticated than iMovie and Movie Maker normally represents a significant investment. Programs such as Avid, Final Cut Pro and Adobe can cost more than a thousand dollars. Like any purchase this large, you'll want to give it a test run before committing.

Sony Vegas Pro

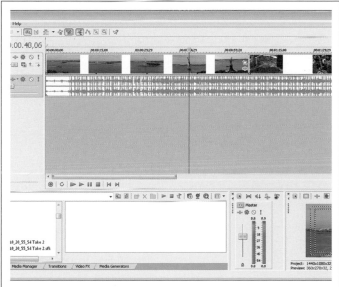

- Sony Vegas Pro is a professional nonlinear editing system designed for Microsoft Windows XP and Vista.

- Originally developed as an audio editor, it eventually developed into an editing program for video and audio.

- Vegas supports unlimited video and audio tracks, any aspect ratio (4:3, 16:9, etc.) and pixel aspect ratio, and any frame rate (23.97, 24, 25, 29.97, 30, etc.).

- Projects can be a mix of source clips with different frame rates and resolutions.

VirtualDub

- VirtualDub is a video capture and video processing utility for Microsoft Windows.

- VirtualDub is free software and mainly geared toward processing AVI video files.

- It lacks the editing power of a general purpose editor,

such as Adobe Premiere, but is streamlined for fast linear operations over video.

- It has batch-processing capabilities for processing large numbers of files that can be extended with third party video filters.

ADVANCED EDITING PROGRAMS
The possibilities are endless when using advanced editing software

Making the decision to invest in video editing software is a commitment. If you plan to edit video on your computer, you're committing to storing and using very large files that will test RAM and push the limits of hard drive space. You'll also need to consider the type of video that you produce, as video for the Web, for home DVDs, and for professional use all have very different requirements.

Professional video software takes the basic features of consumer programs to another level. This is the video software that is used to create many of the movies that we watch in theaters today. It includes the same basic video and audio editing capabilities and expands those functions by making it possible for you to edit and manipulate frame-by-frame.

First and foremost on your list of factors to consider when

Final Cut Pro

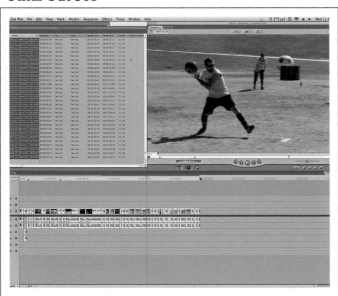

Adobe Premiere Pro

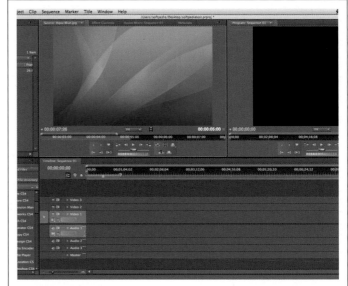

- Final Cut Pro is a professional nonlinear editing software application developed by Apple, Inc.

- It supports an unlimited number of simultaneously composited video tracks; up to ninety-nine audio tracks; and multi-cam editing for cutting video from multiple camera sources, as well as many other standard edit functions.

- It comes with a range of dissolve, iris, distortion, and basic 3D transitions, and a range of video and audio filters such as keying tools, mattes, and vocal de-poppers and de-essers.

- Adobe Premiere Pro is a real-time timeline-based video editing software application.

- It is part of the Adobe Creative Suite, a suite of graphic design, video editing, and Web development applications made by Adobe Systems; it can also be purchased separately.

- Premiere Pro is integrated with Adobe After Effects, an industry standard for motion graphics and compositing. Premiere Pro also integrates well with Adobe Photoshop, whose files can open directly from Premiere Pro.

purchasing a video editing package is your budget. Prices can range from a few hundred dollars to more than the price of a used car. Most software companies offer "lite" versions of their programs that come at a reduced price but at the expense of features. However, the features left out are usually the most advanced features that you might never need.

········· YELLOW ● LIGHT ·········

When you decide on the software you want, search online for the best price. If you buy the software directly from the manufacturer, you have two delivery options: You can download the program directly from their site or have it shipped to you in a box. Downloading the software lets you use it immediately; however, if you spend a few hundred dollars on it, you might like to have a physical copy.

Avid

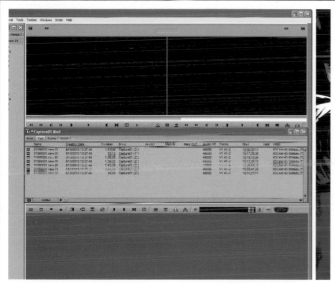

- For most professional film and television editors, there's no substitute for an Avid editing system.

- Avid has been a pioneer in the nonlinear editing industry since 1989 when the company introduced the first version of its Media Composer software.

- Avid is still the industry leader in nonlinear computer-based editing systems. From Oscar-winning films to reality television shows, almost everything is edited on an Avid system.

Find Support

- Technical support is crucial to video editing success.

- Even the most experienced editor encounters problems. When disaster strikes you'll need a place to turn

- Before making a purchase, find out what kind of telephone and online support the software manufacturer offers.

- User forums and blogs are also useful resources when you experience difficulty. It's likely that someone has asked about the same problem before.

- Look online for active, informative support groups before you buy, and you'll know where to go if you have a problem later.

EDITING II

FILE FORMATS: CODECS

The most popular types of file formats and codecs, demystified and explained

Codecs can be intimidating to even an experienced editor. Why? Because there are hundreds, possibly thousands of them, and it is often quite difficult to tell the difference between them. Basically, a video codec is a device or software that enables video compression and/or decompression for digital video. (COmpression + DECompression = CODEC.)

Codecs do compression to reduce file sizes and decompression to make the large video viewable and usable. Most file formats use codecs to help in transferring and storing. Generally, video data must be encoded before it is recorded to the videotape in a camcorder; stored on the hard disk of a computer; burnt on to DVD; transferred over the Internet;

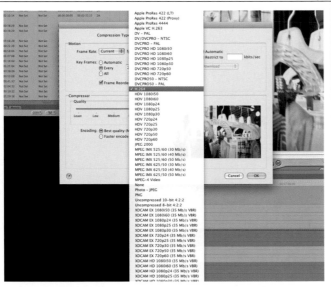

VLC Player

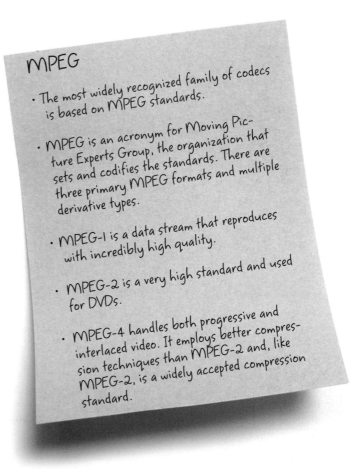

MPEG

- The most widely recognized family of codecs is based on MPEG standards.

- MPEG is an acronym for Moving Picture Experts Group, the organization that sets and codifies the standards. There are three primary MPEG formats and multiple derivative types.

- MPEG-1 is a data stream that reproduces with incredibly high quality.

- MPEG-2 is a very high standard and used for DVDs.

- MPEG-4 handles both progressive and interlaced video. It employs better compression techniques than MPEG-2 and, like MPEG-2, is a widely accepted compression standard.

- If an end user wants to watch a video encoded with a specific codec that is not present and properly installed on the user's computer, the video won't play or won't play correctly.

- Both MPlayer and VLC media player contain many popular codecs in a por- table stand-alone library, available for many operating systems, including Windows, Linux, and Mac OS X.

- Use one of these players to resolve many issues within Windows involving conflicting and poorly installed codecs.

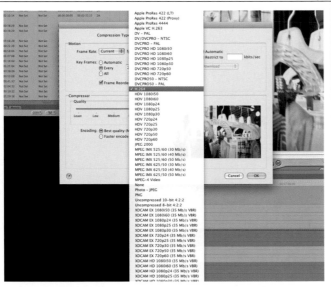

broadcast via satellite or cable; or transferred to a portable device. Then it must be decoded or uncompressed to be played.

Codecs are either lossless or lossy. Most codecs are lossy codecs, which lose varying amounts of information but reproduce the compressed material using less data space. They are great for compressing data that needs to be sent via e-mail or uploaded to the Internet for streaming. Lossless codecs reproduce video exactly as it is without any loss in quality.

Codecs are often designed to emphasize certain aspects of the media, or their use, to be encoded. For example, a digital video of a sports event needs to encode motion well but not necessarily exact colors, while a video of an art exhibit needs to perform well encoding color and surface texture.

When you decide which codec to use, you need to figure out what you want your end result to be. If you first know what you want, then work backward and do a little research on what the pros are doing to get the same results, you'll find the codec that is just right for the job.

H.264

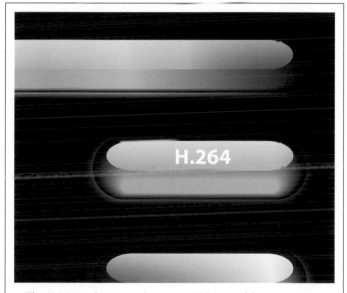

- The H.264 codec is another option for encoding video for Blu-Ray disc, as well as for videos found on iTunes.

- H.264 is a family of standards with great flexibility and a wide variety of applications.

- H.264 enables compression for high and low bit rates and both high and low video resolutions.

- Adjusting size allows users to use this same standard for compressing for broadcast, multimedia usage, and large file storage.

WMV

- Another well-known codec or family of codecs is WMV, which stands for Windows Media Video.

- The most important aspect of a WMV file is that its format allows large video files to be compressed while retaining their high quality.

- WMV 9 is the basis of the SMPTE VC-1 video compression standard, which is another format that can be used for encoding video for Blu-Ray disc.

RENDERING & DVD AUTHORING
Render your movie to your chosen format and burn it to a DVD

Rendering can be one of the most challenging aspects of the digital video post-production process. Rendering involves choosing the final video size, playback speed, and compression. Whether your video will be on the Web or DVD, you have to render. Most current software makes the process easier by choosing the best format for you, but you still need to know the process.

When you edit a project, there are points where you actually change the video image in the clips. For example, when you do a dissolve, one image fades in while the other fades out. This makes a very complex change in the image, which takes a tremendous amount of computing power.

There isn't an all-inclusive guide out there that has all of the rendering answers. Testing is the primary way you can

Real-time Editing

- With real-time video editing, it takes no longer to render a video than the length of that video clip itself.

- Using a real-time system, you can immediately preview your editing work, at full quality, without any rendering delay.

- Computer systems designed for quality real-time video editing employ the highest-quality components, like multiple CPUs.

- Many editing systems have near real-time performance, where rendering is typically real time, except for complex segments.

Preview

- Before you start rendering make sure every video element is lined up the way you want it and ready to go. Check the location of titles, clips, transitions, and effects.

- Preview the playback. Your software will allow you to

play your video, or selected scenes from your movie, in a smaller window.

- Look for any glitches, transition miscues, audio that's slightly out of sync, titles out of alignment, and so forth.

get your render settings just right. You may have to render a video in a few different formats until you find one that works. It is helpful to spend some time researching online about the best render settings for your specific software. Once a file is rendered, you can now upload it to the Web or burn it to a DVD.

Rendering Takes Time

- Rendering is one of the most processor-intensive things your computer can do. One minute of video can take twenty to thirty minutes or longer to render.

- Close down all unnecessary applications. All applications that appear in the task manager that are not system critical should be shut down.

- Minimizing the window may speed it up, but only a little.

- Where possible, render to a disk other than that of the disk where the footage is stored.

Blu-Ray

- There is little point in owning a high-definition camcorder if the video footage needs to be compressed to SD to fit onto a DVD. As more people upgrade to HD televisions and computer monitors, Blu-Ray will become the standard for storing media on optical discs.

- Single layer Blu-Ray discs hold 25GB, about six times the capacity of a DVD, so they are also great for backing up and archiving.

- When choosing a Blu-Ray burner, look for a fast writing speed.

EDITING II

MEDIA MANAGEMENT
A well-organized post-production workflow can help save you time and money

Media management is the process of keeping all the files you will need for video editing accounted for in a system that makes sense. Editors each have their own preferences on how to manage their files, but there are a few things you can do to make the process easier.

Media files, project files, and sharing files are the main types

of files you will work with in video editing. Media files are your actual clips of video or audio. If you shoot an hour of video then capture it into your computer, it becomes a video clip media file. If you record some narration, it becomes an audio clip media file.

The project files are what your edit program creates to tell

File->Save As

- The first thing you should do when you begin a video editing project is launch your software and create a brand new project.

- Immediately do a "save as" of your empty project and

- give it a logical name that will be easy to recognize or remember.

- Save the project file in a specific place that you have set aside for video projects.

Media Bins

- Within video applications, there is another layer of file folders specific to the project itself called bins.

- These folders are not actual file folders; only your video editing program will recognize them.

- Media bins provide a logical structure for projects, making your media easier to manage.

- You can have different bins for voiceovers, titles, A-roll, B-roll, and graphics, among others.

itself all the critical information about the project settings and all of the edit decisions you make.

Project files contain information about where the media files are located. Project files also tell the program how you want those media files manipulated and presented, but they do not contain the media files themselves. The project files can be thought of as a list of detailed information about where your media is stored and what to do with it so that it's edited in the way you want.

When you save your project, you save all your editing decisions and the location of the media files. If you move the location of your media in the middle of an editing project, your editing program will send you a warning message letting you know it's missing the media it needs. It is also important to realize that none of your original media files are actually changed by anything you edit. A sharing file is the video file you create at the very end of an editing project.

Scene Folders

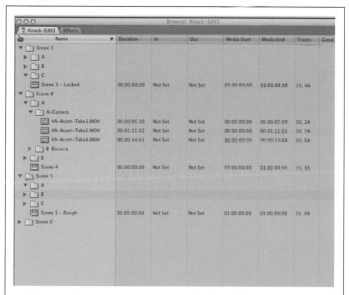

- The way you organize your media files depends largely on the type of project you work on.

- If you edit a long feature film, you would want to create bins by scenes, and sub-level bins for cutaways and camera angles.

- A short video may only need specific bins for locations and dates.

- It is important to avoid storing all of your media files in one large folder.

Filenames

park_16_2

- The names of files should be very specific, yet short enough to be easily identified. Feature film editors often mark filenames with scene number, shot number, and take number. Different camera angles may also be marked if it is a multi-cam shoot.

- Professional video editing software will allow you to add notes to clips, so that more information can be displayed along with the filename.

- For short projects, it may be easier to use simpler filenames.

ASSEMBLING A ROUGH CUT
The first stage in which the film begins to resemble its final product

Once all of your video clips are captured, logged, and orga-nized, you can start putting together a rough cut. This is not meant to be the perfectly assembled end product of the film, but it is the first stage in which the film begins to resemble its final product. Rough cuts do not flow well and still undergo many changes before the release of the film.

After you have looked at all the footage shot and decided

on the best takes, which footage is useful and which is not, you can move the shots into the approximate order they will appear in the final cut.

Once everything is in the proper order, watch the rough cut in its entirety and ask yourself a few questions: Is the story all there? Does it make sense? Are the clips in the best order? If the answer to any question is no, adjust your rough cut until

Editing to Storyboards

- If you're editing a narrative, you should have decided the order of your scenes in pre-production.

- Follow your storyboard and assemble the clips accord-ingly, picking the best take for each scene.

- In the rough cut, you lay down the video and associ-ated audio in the order in which you wish to tell the story, cutting out every-thing that does not move the story forward.

Adding Clips

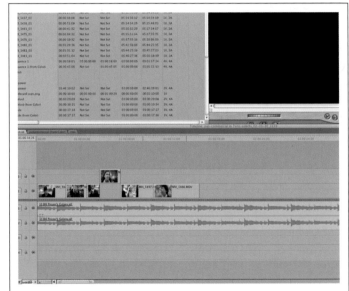

- The most basic way to put clips into sequence is to simply drag them from the project window or from their folder into the video editing timeline.

- The more effective way to bring items into your time-

line is to set "in" and "out" points for a clip.

- Once the clip has its in and out points set, you can drag it to the timeline, and only the part of the video between those points will be copied to the timeline.

the answer is yes. You will cut, watch what you have, make notes about what to change or fix, then do it all over again. This is the real work of the editing process, and there's no one right way to do it.

Keeping Rhythm

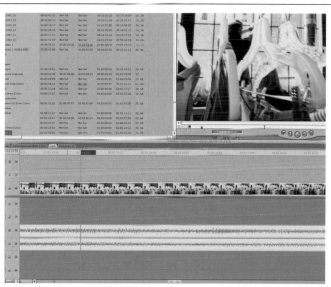

- Good editors will often cut or add as little as a single frame to keep the rhythm of a scene.

- Learning to edit a scene for good rhythm isn't hard, but it can be difficult to master.

- You will likely watch scenes twenty times before you get the rhythm right.

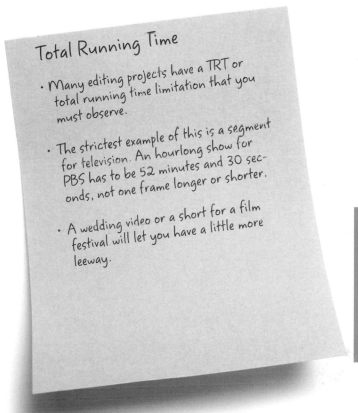

Total Running Time

- Many editing projects have a TRT or total running time limitation that you must observe.

- The strictest example of this is a segment for television. An hourlong show for PBS has to be 52 minutes and 30 seconds, not one frame longer or shorter.

- A wedding video or a short for a film festival will let you have a little more leeway.

SPLIT EDITS

Use these advanced audio/video edit techniques to give your video that polished feel

A split edit essentially bridges two shots with sound. In most edits, the audio and video portions of a scene are cut in sync. The sound and video in a shot begin and end together. In a split edit, the audio track transitions at a different time than the video. The sound from the first of the two clips may continue several seconds after the visual transition has taken place, or the sound from the second clip may begin several seconds before the visual transition takes place. In both cases, sound is used to bridge the two shots.

This technique is used to smooth out edits that might otherwise look and feel abrupt. Almost every editor uses many split edits when editing conversations. In fact, in most

J Cut

- When you want to hear the next shot's audio before you see its video, use a J cut.

- The in point of a clip is adjusted to overlap the preceding clip so that the audio portion of the later clip starts playing before its video.

- A good example of a J cut is when conversation begins as the scene dissolves to the characters engaged in mid-meal dialogue.

L Cut

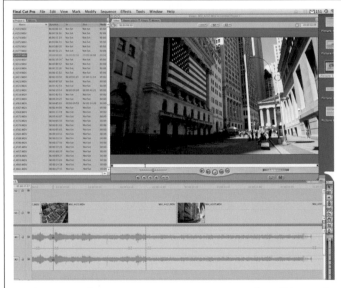

- The L cut is the opposite of a J cut; the audio out point of a clip is extended beyond the video out point, so that the audio cuts after the video and continues playing over the beginning of the next clip.

- L cuts are often used during a conversation where one person may be talking and the picture switches to someone else listening to them.

- It's called an "L" cut because when editing, the sound and picture are cut into two separate points, which creates an L shape on the timeline.

dialogue scenes you see, every cut is a split edit.

A split edit should have some sort of motivation to it, regardless of the type of production. If you cut a scene that is driven more by narrative, like a dialogue scene in a film, you will look for moments of unspoken or nonverbal feelings to motivate the split edit. You need to look for logical places to make your cut. With some experience, you will get better at choosing the location for a split edit that makes sense to both you and your audience.

By experimenting with variations of the split edit, with audio leading video and vice versa, you will discover a variety of exciting ways to add interest to your productions. By adjusting the length of the transitions, you can experiment and see for yourself what works and what doesn't. Split edits are satisfying when you see the effect they have on a production.

B-roll

- Often used in interviews and documentaries, B-roll is supplemental or alternate footage that is intercut with the main footage.

- B-roll is usually video only, and it is most often used over the A-roll audio, in place of the A-roll video.

- B-roll is also called "safety footage" or "backup footage." It can save your project by covering a jump cut caused when you need to cut that sneeze or nose-mining segment out.

- Split edits can make your video flow smoothly between A-roll and B-roll.

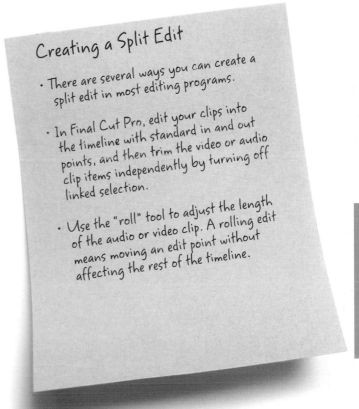

Creating a Split Edit

- There are several ways you can create a split edit in most editing programs.

- In Final Cut Pro, edit your clips into the timeline with standard in and out points, and then trim the video or audio clip items independently by turning off linked selection.

- Use the "roll" tool to adjust the length of the audio or video clip. A rolling edit means moving an edit point without affecting the rest of the timeline.

VHS TO DIGITAL
Besides being obsolete, VHS tape quality degrades with time

Now is the time to convert VHS to digital and start enjoying those home movies in a more convenient format that will preserve your cherished moments far better than analog tapes. Move your memories into the twenty-first century, clean out that tape storage area, recycle that old VHS deck, and say goodbye to the hassle of VHS forever.

Copying your old videos to a DVD or your computer is not that difficult, as long as you have the proper equipment. The first step requires connecting the VCR or camcorder to the computer through a common interface. You'll need either a video card that can take a VCR's video and audio as input, or a video tuner card that can tune to the TV channel that the VCR broadcasts on. The most advanced video-out port on a VHS tape deck is the S-Video port. If the deck does not

Old Tapes

- Do you want your memories sitting in a box somewhere on a medium that degrades with every playback and over time?

- VHS tapes and VCRs are fast becoming an obsolete technology.

- Convert VHS to digital

- files now to preserve your memories safely.

- VCRs are still available, as are services and machines that help you convert your VHS tapes to DVD. If you continue to wait, you'll see fewer opportunities to make this change and save your VHS footage.

Connecting Your Camcorder

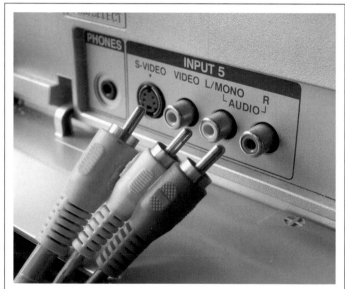

- Another way of converting analog (VHS, Hi8, etc.) tape to digital signal format is through your digital camcorder.

- Use the S-Video or composite cables to connect the wires from the VCR's out to the camcorder's in.

- With the VCR deck wired to your camcorder, you can now make the connection from the digital camcorder to the computer. This is typically done with a FireWire (IEEE-1394) connection.

have S-Video out, it will have composite video out. Since neither video port carries audio, the deck will also have two RCA audio-out ports for a stereo signal. In the streaming process, choose a standard National Television System Committee (NTSC) capture rate of 29.97 frames per second, and a resolution that is at least as great as the original resolution.

ZOOM

If you don't have a video capture card, there are several products that can be purchased to interface your VCR with the computer. Perhaps the easiest way to convert VHS to digital in this case is to buy an A/V-to-USB adapter cable. This cable features a USB connector on one end, and at the other end, an S-Video connector, a composite video connector, and two RCA audio connectors.

Video Capture Card

- Most desktop video capture cards include an S-Video in port for accepting streaming media, along with a 3.5mm stereo line-in port.

- An S-Video cable can be run from the tape deck to the capture card. The capture card should also have composite-in, if S-Video is unavailable on the deck.

- An RCA audio cable can be purchased that has left/right connectors on one end, and a 3.5mm male stereo connector on the other, to connect the audio.

VHS to DVD

- Once you have the files in digital form on your computer, you can edit them the way you would any other digital file and then burn them directly to DVD.

- If you don't want to edit and just want to make DVD copies of your VHS movies, you can buy a DVD/VHS recorder.

- All you have to do is insert a blank DVD and the original tape, press the copy button, and walk away.

EDITING TECHNIQUES

PAN & ZOOM IMAGES
Use this technique to add life to otherwise still images

Telling stories with images is an activity that people have engaged in since photographs became commonplace. The advent of the digital camera means that more complex narratives can be built around digital photographs, with users taking advantage of a computer's abilities to edit, copy, and enhance images with text, sound, and even with motion. Software is available to help users tell stories with their digital

photos. You can do all this and much more with the Pan and Zoom effect (also known as the Ken Burns effect). The technique is principally used in historical documentaries where film or video material is not available.

You can emphasize the wide expanse of a panorama by sweeping across the photograph from left to right, or you can slowly scan the camera across each person in a group photo.

Ken Burns

- In the documentary series, *Civil War,* Ken Burns made extensive use of more than 16,000 archival photographs, paintings, and newspaper images.

- The Pan and Zoom effect was not created by Ken Burns, but his films are

generally where people first observed the power of using moving stills in a video project.

- Ken Burns' other documentaries *Jazz, Baseball,* and *Thomas Jefferson* also make use of this effect.

Pan and Zoom

- Unless you're after a special effect, avoid very fast pans and zooms. It's better to go slowly to allow your viewers to absorb the changes in the scene.

- Use images at least 800×600 in size. The bigger the image and higher the resolution, the more

you can zoom in without introducing distortion and pixilation.

- This is especially true if you work in a high-definition format. You may find that you can't zoom in very far on photos that have a relatively low resolution.

That great expression on a person's face can be highlighted by zooming in on it. Creative use of zooming can help tell your story. When you zoom in, you gradually focus the viewer's attention on one portion of the scene. You tell the viewer, "This is the part of the picture that you should pay attention to." When you zoom out, you reveal additional details about the scene, increasing the viewer's sense of context.

Ken Burns Effect

- The Ken Burns effect name was used by Apple in 2003 for a feature in its iMovie software.

- iMovie makes it easy to apply a Pan and Zoom effect, but lacks the control you can achieve with other programs.

- With other programs such as Final Cut Pro, you have to set key frames for position, scale, and center parameters under the motion tab.

Pan and Zoom in Video

- You can also use the Pan and Zoom effect on video clips.

- You can use this effect to zoom in slightly on a video that was originally filmed as a locked shot.

- If the camera panned during filming, but you would like a more sweeping movement in your final video, use Pan and Zoom to sweep across the width of the video frame while the camera is also panning.

- This can produce a truly dramatic feeling of fast movement.

EDITING TECHNIQUES

ASPECT RATIOS
Different videos have different aspect ratios—this can cause trouble

The aspect ratio is the width of a picture in relationship to its height. The three most common ratios are 4:3, 16:9, and 2.39:1, although there are several other ratios used in different countries and at different times. Whether the television screen is seven inches or forty-two inches, the aspect ratio doesn't change regardless of the actual physical dimensions of the image.

When television first came along, it adopted the aspect ratio of 4:3, so that it could easily show previously recorded motion pictures. This is why standard-definition TVs and older computer monitors use this aspect ratio.

After the advent of TV, motion picture directors began experimenting with wider aspect ratios to get people interested in returning to the theaters. Typically, these films came

4:3

- 4:3 means that the picture is four units wide for every three units of height. The width is 1.33 times as large as the height.

- A video with dimensions of 320 x 240 pixels has an aspect ratio of 4:3. 640 x 480 video also has an aspect ratio of 4:3. The two

video clips can have totally different sizes but share the same aspect ratio.

- Standard televisions and camcorders that shoot a 4:3 ratio will become obsolete as more and more TV stations shift to HD programming.

16:9

- 16:9 is the newly accepted default format for wide-screen TV, DVD, and high-definition video.

- The horizontal orientation is more akin to how your eyes view objects.

- The great width of 16:9 gives you more room to tell your story and to have multiple stories going on in the same frame without crowding one another.

- In a 4:3, you might have to cut between two shots that you can fit in the same frame in 16:9.

to television in a truncated 4:3 format. Sometimes they used a technique known as pan and scan, where only a section of the entire image would pan back and forth across the widescreen images to keep the center of interest on the television screen.

Later, as TV screens got larger, letterboxing came into style, maintaining the widescreen formatting of the original by placing black bars at the top and bottom of the TV screen and showing the image full width.

21:9

- CinemaScope is a very wide screen format often used for theatrical release movies. *The Robe* was the first film to use this format.

- The CinemaScope image was photographed on standard 35mm film with an anamorphic lens.

- When projected in the cinema through another anamorphic lens, it produced a ratio of 2.35:1 and a screen size that was two and a half times the size of the conventional screen aspect ratio of 1.33:1.

- Actual ratios can vary from 2.39:1 to 2.55:1.

Aspect Ratio Conversion

- The problem of converting pictures between different formats has plagued film and television companies for years.

- Conversions almost always involve compromise and often annoy the audience, the film director, or both.

- Changing the aspect ratio of a video can make people look distorted, either too narrow or too wide.

- Simply crop the top and bottom of a video shot in 4:3 to make it 16:9 (cropped area shown by black fill), or crop sides off of 16:9 images for a 4:3 image.

AUDIO POST OVERVIEW

Sweeten up your sound while also adding music, ambiance, and sound effects

Audio post-production work begins once you have a locked cut of the film. The locked cut is the film in its final visual form. No further alterations to the look of the film are made beyond this point.

Once you have your film locked, you can begin spotting it for the placement of sound effects and music. Every scene in

your project should be evaluated from the point of view of how audio can be best used to enhance and help the story.

Spotting for music is the process of viewing the locked cut and deciding where the music score will be. Spotting for sound requires determining if and where any dialogue problems exist; where sound effects will be needed; and if any

Dialogue Editing

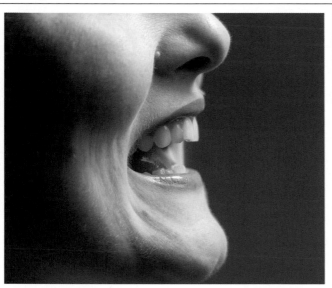

- Take time to go through your video and examine every single line of spoken dialogue.

- Listen for badly recorded lines or times when an actor's voice is out of sync with his lips.

- Dialogue should be clear enough that you can easily make out every word without effort.

- Remember, viewers can close their eyes, but they can't close their ears.

Spotting for Sound

- Watch your locked cut from beginning to end a few times before spotting for sound.

- Write down the time code of any instances where your project needs additional audio work.

- It may be helpful to get another person's input during this stage.

- You have become so familiar with your project that it may be easy for you to understand what an actor is saying, while someone watching it for the first time may not.

sound design will be required.

During the mix, the edited production dialogue and ADR, sound effects, and musical elements that will comprise the soundtrack are assembled in their edited form, and balanced to become the final soundtrack.

Making badly recorded audio sound good is one thing that cannot be done in audio post-production. Certain techniques will help you make bad audio sound better, but it won't be able to be completely fixed. Take the time to record good audio during production.

Audio Syncing

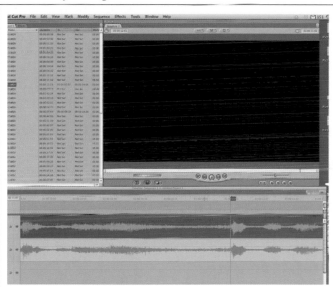

- Synchronization of sound and video quickly becomes an issue when editing. It helps to make a distinction between the audio elements that must stay in absolute sync with the video and those that do not need to.

- On-screen dialogue and sound effects that coincide with on-screen action require exact synchronization with the video.

- Off-camera dialogue, dialogue shot with the mouth not visible, background music, background ambiance, and certain sound effects do not need to be synced.

Audio File Formats

- There are a number of different types of audio files. The type is usually determined by the file extension (what comes after the "." in the filename). For example, ".wav," ".mp3," or ".dct."

- WAV: standard audio file format used mainly in Windows PCs. Commonly used for storing uncompressed, CD-quality sound files that can be large in size.

- MP3: the MPEG Layer-3 format is the most popular format for downloading and storing music.

- Other popular formats are WMA, OGG, and AAC.

POST-PRODUCTION

AUDIO LEVELS

You can adjust audio levels to achieve a cleaner, more even sounding dialogue

If you actively listen to your recorded tracks, you'll start hearing all the additional noises that you recorded. If you want the audience to hear these clips clearly, spend some time adjusting the audio levels of your clips so that they're more or less consistent. The concept of a balanced audio signal can be difficult to grasp since you can't see sound. Once you get your audio inside the computer, it is easier to see. The first thing you'll notice when you open a sound file in your editing program is a center zero line with information above and below the line. If you zoom in a little bit you'll see that the audio waveform is evenly distributed in the upper and lower regions. This is a balanced audio signal.

dB Meter

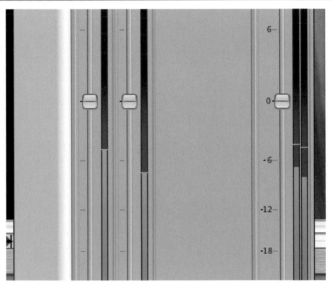

- Unless all your footage comes from the same source and the same setup, the audio levels you've recorded will probably vary greatly from clip to clip.

- Spend some time adjusting the audio levels of your

clips so that they play at consistent volume throughout your video.

- Your audience will be able to hear your film's sound more clearly without dramatic changes in volume.

Audio Compression

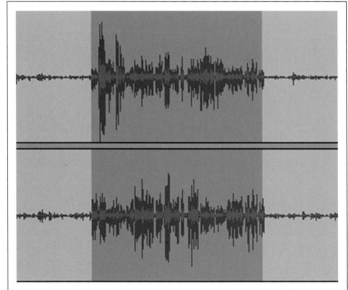

- Compression reduces the dynamic range of an audio signal. It narrows the difference between high and low audio levels or volumes, reducing the level of loud sounds and lifting the level of quiet ones.

- It will make it so the audience can hear an actor's

whisper just as well as it can hear a gunshot or explosion.

- Compression is applied to nearly every form of audio you hear, from radio and television broadcasting to music production.

Using the zero line as a reference point, the audio contains equal amounts of positive and negative information. This is seen in the movement of the woofers in your PC, home, or car stereo speakers. With no signal, the woofer cone sits in a neutral, or zero position. When audio is played through the speaker, the woofer travels forward and backward in response to the positive and negative portions of the audio signal.

Audio Normalization

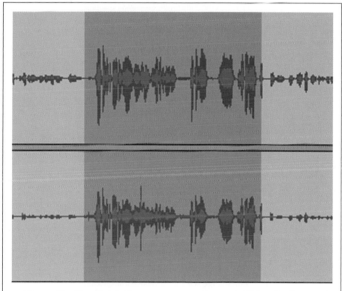

- Normalization finds the highest peak in your track and raises that to whatever setting you are normalizing to (usually 0 dB).

- For example, if the highest peak in your track is -2 dB, normalizing to 0 dB will raise everything in the track by 2 dB.

- Before cutting and mixing multiple audio sources together, you may need to normalize varying audio levels that are intended to match.

Graphic EQ

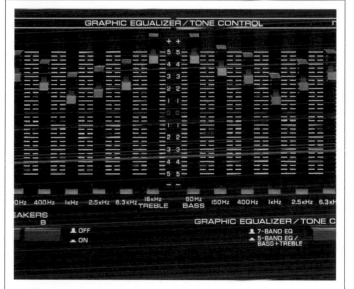

- All sounds cover a certain range of frequencies. When a sound is too strong or too weak in one frequency area, it won't sound right.

- An EQ, or equalizer, lets you boost or cut specific frequency ranges, which will help make out-of-balance audio sound better.

- If a microphone sounds dull, removing the low midrange can clean up the sound.

- If an actor was too far from his mic, bringing up the bass can restore some of the missing warmth in the sound.

SOUND EFFECTS
Adding sound effects to your movie gives it an extra punch

Once you have the dialogue and voiceover tracks edited and sounding good, the next step is to add secondary sounds, such as ambiance and sound effects. Sound effects have immense value in video production.

In feature film production, almost none of the original sound recorded during the shoot ends up in the final version. In a scene where a couple is eating at an outdoor café,

the only sounds recorded on the day of the shoot that make it into the final cut are the actors' dialogue. The outside ambiance, traffic noise, sounds of other diners, clanking of dishes, and drinking and chewing of food are all added in post-production.

If you can't find an effect that works for you in a sound effects library, you can make your own. These homemade

Sound Effects Library

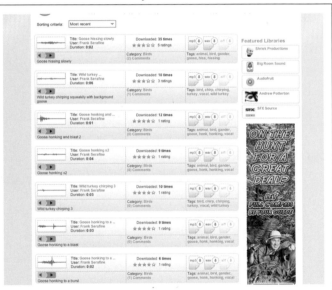

- There are hundreds of sound effects libraries available to purchase or download online.

- If you only need a few effects, you may be able to find what you need online for free. However, these

effects are usually of lower quality.

- Sometimes, just browsing through the index of available sounds can spark some creative ideas on how you can add new interest to your project.

Recording

- To record footsteps, place your camcorder on a tripod close to a hard floor.

- Point the microphone at the subject and use shoes or boots to make a series of footstep sounds.

- Capture the audio into your editing program and sync the sound.

- It may help to loop the video sequence on a monitor while recording so you can match the footsteps exactly.

types of effects can be divided into two categories: found and created. Found effects are those that you can get easily by re-recording the item itself, such as door slams, car engines, dogs barking, etc. Created sounds are those you'll need to create because recording the live item is too dangerous or impossible, such as an earthquake or bomb blasts.

Telephone Effect

- You can use most editing programs to easily make audio for which you already have recorded sound like a phone call.

- Use the high pass and low pass filter, or the equalizer, to remove all frequencies below 300 hertz and those above 300 hertz.

- This closely emulates what happens to sound over a real telephone connection.

- If the source audio is stereo, convert it to mono as well.

Witness Protection Effect

- If an interview subject wants to remain anonymous, you will have to alter his voice.

- A common technique for this is to mix the regular track of his voice with a pitch-adjusted track.

- You can shift the pitch down a few semi-tones, making the voice sound deeper, or up a few semi-tones, making the voice sound like a chipmunk.

ADR & NARRATION

If you didn't capture good sound while on set, you can rerecord it in post

Automated dialogue replacement, or ADR for short, is the process of rerecording replacement dialogue for a production. ADR is used for many reasons. The most common use of ADR is to replace noisy audio recorded on the day of the shoot. Rerecording lines is done to obtain clean sound or to subtly adjust an actor's performance in a scene by having an actor deliver the same line with a slightly different inflection. It can also be used to add new non-sync dialogue to help the story.

ADR techniques can eliminate profanity for a television audience or completely replace voices for use in another country. Television and movies showcase ADR all the time.

Recording ADR

- Professional ADR is done in a sound booth so the recording is as clean and echo free as possible.

- If you don't have access to a sound booth, record your ADR in the quietest, echo-free space available.

- You can improvise a sound booth by draping some heavy blankets around the microphone position. Better yet, record your ADR in the smallest closet available, with the clothes still hanging in it.

- Ideally, you should use the same microphone that was used on the set.

Recording Narration

- Doing a great voiceover starts with a great script. Your script should be clean and easy to read.

- Record several versions of your narration, changing word or phrase emphasis and speed. This way you can decide later which version works best.

- Preface each recording with the project name and take number to make it easier to navigate when editing the narration together.

Feature-length movies, TV dramas, reality programming, and even animation and video games all use ADR at one time or another.

ADR is used extensively on big budget films, since it is almost impossible to get clean sound on a set where several hundred people may be working. But ADR is also extremely valuable for independent films where you don't have full control of the location and therefore may end up with unwanted background noise in your sound.

Editing Narration

- Once the ADR work is loaded into your editing software, go through all your takes, select the best parts, and copy them into a new project.

- Once you have a rough cut of your narration, go through it and remove any unwanted noises.

- Look for times when the narrator took in a deep breath, stuttered, or mispronounced a word.

- Add and subtract the silence in between words and phrases until the narration sounds natural.

Plosives and Sibilance

- Plosives occur when humans speak words that require a complete closure of the mouth, such as words with B, P, or T sounds

- Sibilance is an excess of high frequencies created by S and T sounds.

- You can eliminate plosives and sibilance during the recording by using a windscreen a few inches from your microphone or speaking into the microphone at a slightly off-center angle.

- Plosives can be eliminated in post-production by applying a high pass filter, and sibilance can be fixed by using a de-esser. Most audio editing software has these filters built in.

POST-PRODUCTION

MUSIC

If used correctly and timed right, music has a profound effect on the audience's mood

Music has the power to comfort, entertain, inspire, relax, unnerve, and even intimidate. Try to listen closely for the music tracks when you watch television programs and movies. The music will often creep in quietly, unnoticed by the viewer. The music builds as the emotions heighten. When you use video and music together correctly, you can express to your audience exactly how you want them to feel.

All types of video benefit from the addition of music. Some videos, like music videos and montage sequences, may not have any sound besides a music track. Mix the music low in videos with dialogue or narration so it doesn't interfere.

Make your film look and feel like a real motion picture by

Pirating Music

- Beware of pirating music: Even if you only want to post your video on YouTube .com, having an audio track that you do not have permission to use can get your video muted or pulled from the site.

- Popular music has its own cultural connotations,

which means that viewers have preconceived opinions on the music's meaning.

- You are usually better off using good original music that is new to your audience.

Local Band

- Many local and college bands would love the opportunity to have their music appear in your film.

- Work out a written agreement with the band where you use a few tracks in your film and in return put the band's name in your credits, promotion on your Web

site, provide them with a copy of the film when finished, etc.

- There also are many musicians and small bands online that would have no problem allowing you to use their music in your project.

adding in a quality soundtrack. On a limited budget, however, it can be very difficult to get the exact type of music you want for your film. Using a popular song from a big time band will not be possible unless you have a huge budget, as you need to pay for the use of the song.

License fees—fees paid out to the record companies for rights to use a song—can be staggering and are determined based on various factors, including how the music is used, the duration and number of times the music is used, and where the film will be performed. Student films that are only shown within an educational environment can often negotiate reduced fees. Independent filmmakers planning to show their films at festivals often can also negotiate a reduced fee, called a festival use license. These reduced rates are based on limited screenings of the film. Once the film has been sold for theatrical release, the fees will rise based on the significant increase in viewership and potential increased revenues.

Royalty-free Music

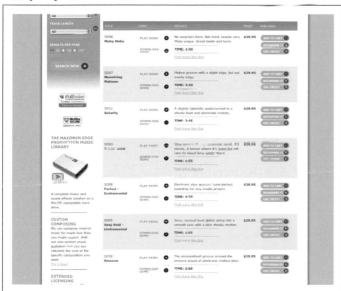

- With royalty-free music, you pay a one-time fee and get rights to unlimited use of a track or all of the tracks in the library.

- Royalty-free music is tailored for specific genres, such as commercials, weddings, or corporate videos.

- Since royalty-free music tracks are a predetermined length, they may not fit as well into your project as would a custom-made track.

- Don't edit your video to fit the royalty-free track; this brings too much attention to the music, which can sometimes be subpar.

Make Your Own Music

- If you have a musical background, you can try to compose your own track.

- If you can't play music, chances are that you know someone who does.

- The two most common types of instruments people play are the piano and the guitar, both of which are often used in film scoring.

AUDIO PROGRAMS

There are many choices in audio editing software, from free to ultra-expensive

Sound editors use computerized editing systems called digital audio workstations (DAW). DAWs are multi-track systems that greatly simplify and enhance the sound editing process for all types of professional audio production.

DAWs vary greatly in size, price, and complexity. The most basic systems are simply software applications that can be loaded onto a standard personal computer. Besides multiple dialogue tracks, an editor can add dozens of background effects and layers of Foley and music. Multiple tracks can be cut, copied, pasted, trimmed, and faded at once; each track comes with dozens of controls for volume, stereo panning, and effects, which greatly simplifies the mixing process.

Pro Tools

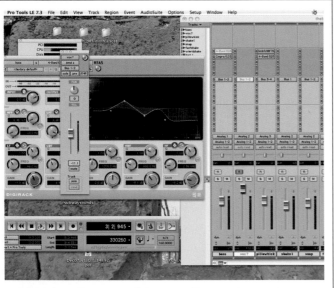

- Pro Tools is the most widely used software system for professional audio recording and editing.

- Pro Tools capabilities include recording and editing music tracks, recording vocals and instruments, multi-tracking, removing background noise, mixing, special effects, and mastering.

- Pro Tools also is used by professionals for recording and editing in music production and film scoring.

- Pro Tools is difficult to learn and expensive. It is compatible with Macintosh and Windows.

Audacity

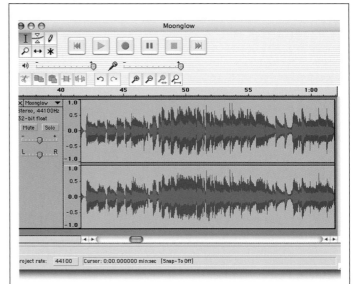

- Free DAW software varies from very basic to advanced. Some programs are easy to use while others take time to learn.

- Audacity is a free software, cross-platform digital audio editor, and recording application—the most popular one available.

- Look for an editing program that is compatible with today's most popular file formats, such as MP3, WAV, AIFF, and OGG.

- Be sure to read reviews online before you download or buy any software.

The heart of your DAW system is your computer, whether Mac or PC. The computer and its subsystems (CPU, RAM, hard drives, etc.) will determine how many tracks you can record and play at once, how many plug-ins you can apply in real time, how long edits will take, and so on.

Plug-ins can extend the capability of the running programs. Plug-ins can be processors, such as compressors, limiters, equalizers, amp/speaker simulators, or effects, like delay, reverb, chorus, and so on. They can be virtual instruments, software synthesizers, or samplers.

GarageBand

- GarageBand is a streamlined DAW and music sequencer that can record and play back multiple tracks of audio. The program is used by independent filmmakers to compose music by putting together looped audio.

- GarageBand comes with the iLife suite of applications that comes included on new Macintosh computers.

- While GarageBand is only available for Macs, there are similar programs available for Windows machines, such as Sony Acid and FL Studio.

Audio in Editing Software

- If you don't want to use a standalone DAW, you can do basic audio editing in most video editing programs.

- Generally, you will have less control when editing audio with video editing software, but you will still be able to apply basic effects, adjust the volume, pitch, etc. Some editing programs are quite good at editing audio and may be all you need. Sony Vegas Pro, for example, started off as an audio program and eventually turned into a video editing program. It features editing on unlimited tracks, plug-in support, and over thirty customizable real-time audio effects.

USING EFFECTS
When and where should you use effects in your film?

Special effects (or SFX) are used in the film and entertainment industry to create effects that cannot be achieved by normal means, such as travel to other star systems. They are also used when creating the effect by normal means is too expensive, such as an enormous explosion.

Many different visual special effects techniques exist, ranging from traditional theater effects to classic film techniques invented in the early twentieth century to modern computer graphics techniques. Often several different techniques are used together in a single scene or shot to achieve the desired effect.

The fairy tale, ethereal nature of film is enhanced by realistic effects. Crashes, planets, jumps, and monsters must be both spectacular and believable.

Pre-conceived Effects

- One reason to use an effect would be for a preconceived creative choice, such as placing your actor in another location or adding an explosion.

- These effects are often essential to your story and must be carefully planned during pre-production.

- The secret of any effect lies in selling it with supporting shots. For example, a car crash will need high-speed shots of the cars, close-ups of the drivers, and shots after the crash.

Fixing Problems

- Another reason that you would use effects is to fix a problem with your video.

- Bad performances, incorrect eye lines, clearance issues, digital dropouts, focal problems, off-tilt tripods, and color timing shifts can all be fixed using special effects and filters.

- Some filmmakers feel every shot they captured with a camera can be improved in post-production.

- Although some things can be easily fixed in post, others cannot. If you get it right on the set, you'll be much happier with the end results.

Some effects are classic and great for almost any video. Others are childish, tacky, or just plain strange, and using them will mark your video as an amateur production. Great effects should only complement the overall story and never call attention to themselves. If the effect causes the viewer to notice the effect more than the idea it is supposed to support, then it shouldn't be used.

············· GREEN ● LIGHT ··············

Keep an eye out for special effects while watching television and movies. Doing this will give you ideas on how to use creative effects in your own work. The best effects are the ones that are often so subtle that only you and other filmmakers will notice them. The average viewer will get a feel that something cool just happened but not really know why.

In-camera Effects

- Most camcorders will come with some effects built in. Most times these effects should not be used.

- It is always better to add your effects in post-production instead of to your raw video.

- If you use the black and white effect in your camcorder's effects menu to record video, that footage will be stuck black and white forever.

Movies Notable for Special Effects

- 2001: A Space Odyssey (1968): The movie pioneered many special effects, too many to list.

- Tron (1982): This was the first computer imagery used to create a 3D world, making it one of the pioneering CGI (computer-generated image) films.

- Cliffhanger (1993): The ability to erase wires changed how stunts are done.

- Forrest Gump (1994): While most filmmakers in the early 1990s used digital effects to create fantasy, the creators of this movie altered history.

- Jurassic Park (1993): This introduced CGI live animals with realistic movements and believable textured muscles and skin.

PRACTICAL EFFECTS

Many practical effects haven't changed since film's early days and are still in use today

Practical effects are those that are done using props or special gear to produce an effect. No trick photography or post-production editing is used. Practical effects include weather effects, water effects, and pyrotechnics. Stunts, bullet hits, explosions, collapsing buildings, breakaway furniture, walls or windows, and tilting or shaking platforms under the set are also considered practical effects. Many of the effects used in action movies are practical effects. Practical effects also are referred to as physical, special, or mechanical effects.

Animatronics are powered by pumps, motors, hydraulics, computers, or other electronic or mechanical means and may be preprogrammed or remotely controlled. The device

Fake Blood

- There are many ways to concoct fake blood, ranging from edible blood made from kitchen ingredients to chemically mixed, realistic blood used on movie sets.

- Feature films that have access to a licensed pyro technician use explosive squibs to simulate a gunshot.

- Be creative. You can fill a small plastic bag with fake blood, tape it under your clothes, and smash it with your hands or run a small garden sprayer under your shirt and spray red colored liquid through it.

Nuclear Bomb Flash

- You can easily simulate the flash of light from a nuclear bomb using your camera's manual iris setting.

- If you open the iris all the way rapidly it will fill the screen with a bright light lasting a few seconds.

- The iris setting can produce other effects when set to underexpose or overexpose images.

may only perform a limited range of movements or it may be incredibly versatile.

In the field of special effects, a miniature effect is a special effect generated by the use of scale models. The use of scale models started in the earliest days of film. A lot of big productions still use them in conjunction with computer effects. *Independence Day, Titanic, The Lord of the Rings* trilogy, and *The Dark Knight* utilized miniatures for a large part of their visual effects work.

Special effects makeup is any makeup process; it includes animatronics and prosthetics. Prosthetic effects include the attachment of false limbs and features or other large pieces that are attached to actors.

Physical effects are often quite dangerous for stunt performers and the technicians who operate them. Working with stunt coordinators, the physical effects crew must devise ways to make stunts as safe as possible. Breakaway glass and furniture let a stunt performer smash through a window. Fires must be safe and containable. Explosions, whether small or large, should be left to professionals.

Altering Perception

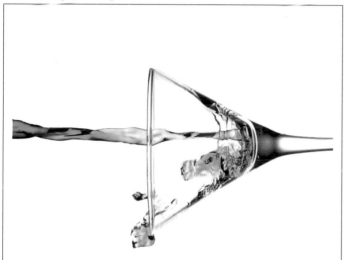

- You can simplify the appearance of zero gravity for liquids and objects simply by turning your camera upside down and sideways.

- If you turn the camera sideways and upside down and fill a glass with liquid, it will make the liquid appear to fly horizontally across the screen.

- Altering perception is an effect that can work well in commercials, music videos, and science fiction movies.

Cling Wrap Filter

- You can make a cheap soft focus filter to give your video a hazy dreamlike quality using household items.

- Stretch a piece of cling wrap tight over the lens of your camcorder and attach it with a rubber band. Make sure the cling wrap is tight enough so it doesn't shift while shooting.

- You can add a little baby oil to the makeshift cling wrap cover to produce different effects.

COMPOSITING

Compositing is the process of layering one image on another to create a single image

Compositing is the process of layering several different clips of video, still images, text, or other graphical elements over one another to create a single on-screen image. Compositing is everywhere. It would be almost impossible to watch a movie or an hour of television and not see some sort of compositing.

Compositing isn't nearly as tough as you might think. Since

it blends two images together for a brief moment, a dissolve is a composite for whatever duration the transition lasts. Adding titles and graphics is compositing.

To start compositing, you will need to work with two or more video layers on your timeline. Put some kind of static or moving image on video track two with some sort of

Blur

- Today's video editing programs offer dozens of blur effects.

- You have the choice to add a simple blur, motion blurs, Gaussian blurs, ripple blurs, wind blurs, and dozens of other types.

- You will have control over the parameters of the blur such as direction, amount, opacity, and duration.

- You can apply a blur inside of a matte to selectively blur only part of a video image to produce many different types of effects.

Opacity

- You can achieve many different effects by adjusting the opacity of an image.

- By default the opacity of your video is 100 percent or completely opaque (visible).

- As you reduce the opacity of a video track, it becomes

more transparent and the track below becomes more visible. If there is no track underneath, the black background becomes visible.

- You can give a person a ghost-like appearance by reducing his opacity to around 30 percent.

transparency and you will be able to see through to video track one. That's it.

Sometimes beginners get confused because they simply stack two clips on top of one another in their timeline. The result is not a composite, but a regular single image. The problem is that if both scenes are full screen, the picture on the highest track will block any scene behind it. In order to create a composite, the top clip must be manipulated to allow the clip below it to show through.

Another concept important to compositing is the use of mattes. Mattes are the electronic equivalent of cutting a shape out of a piece of construction paper and holding it over a picture. If you use the hole in the paper as the matte, the background image shows through the hole. If you use the cutout piece, you block the background picture with the shape of the cutout. The mattes in your editing software work the same way.

Garbage Matte

- A garbage matte removes unneeded portions of the scene, resulting in a rough area that contains only the subject that you want to keep.

- When you work with a poorly lit or uneven blue or green screen, using a garbage matte around the subject can reduce the amount of work that you have to do in keying out the background.

- Garbage mattes are very easy to use and available in most all video editing programs.

Film Look

- Getting your video to look like film is mostly achieved during production by using proper lighting and camera techniques, but there are certain effects you can apply in post-production that will help.

- Reducing the color intensity may make your video look more like film.

- You can download certain plug-ins, such as the Magic Bullet suite, that are especially designed to give your video a more film-like look.

185

COLOR CORRECTION
Color correcting your video can really give it a good look

Before your video is completed, it should be color corrected scene by scene so that the shots match perfectly. Color correction enhances or creates the overall look of your film or video. In other cases, it is used to fix exposure and lighting problems on the set.

Many past directors controlled color on the set with lighting and costume, but filmmakers today, with the advancement of computerized post-production techniques, opt to control color with editing software.

Most color correction is supposed to be subtle, such as bringing down the whites to levels that are suitable for broadcast, correcting under or overexposure, or even correcting a white balance problem.

Though the process of color correction is slightly different

Adjusting White Balance

- You can change the white balance of your video in post-production if you did not properly white balance while shooting, or if you just want to change it to get a different look.

- Most editing software has multiple filters that let you

alter the white balance with just a few clicks.

- The program offers default white balance settings, such as warming or cooling, or allows you to adjust the white balance manually.

Adjusting Hue

- Another way to tint a video is to create a solid-color matte, place it on a track above your video clip, and reduce its opacity.

- A popular effect that is used extensively in TV and movies is to adjust the overall tint and hue of a

video to give it a specific feel. Orange and blue are commonly used.

- You also can isolate colors and enhance them to form effects such as those seen in films like *Sin City* and *Pleasantville*.

in each program, the general idea is mostly the same. Most software offers a color correction filter and a three-way color corrector filter. These are the most versatile and commonly used filters for color grading. You should first concentrate on adjusting the video's contrast, then work on its color balance. The eye is more sensitive to changes in contrast than to differences in color, so this is the best place to start.

MAKE IT EASY

The three-way color corrector filter is a visual interface that has three color wheels with luminance sliders beneath them, along with other controls. While the color correction filter lets you adjust the overall color balance of a clip, the three-way filter gives you even more control by allowing you to adjust the color balance of the shadows, midtones, and highlights individually.

High Contrast

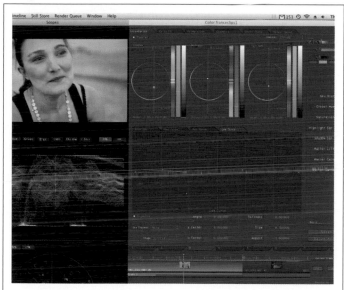

Black and White

- The three-way color corrector filter allows you to individually adjust the color balance of the shadows, midtones, and highlights of an image.

- High contrast scenes are often used for flashbacks and dream sequences, as well as a stylized look.

- Every editing program has a different way to handle primary and secondary color correction. The best way to learn is to open up the software and experiment with different settings and adjustments.

- A black and white effect can be used for only part of a project for a flashback, or for the entire project to give it a classic feel.

- Instead of using the one-click black and white button in your software, use the color correction option

to lower the saturation all the way.

- You can give your video a partially black and white look by adjusting the saturation until you get the color consistency you are looking for.

CHROMA KEY: GREEN SCREEN

Place yourself anywhere in the universe by standing in front of a green screen

The ability to replace a background with another image is a commonly used special effect. Chroma key refers to shooting the subject in front of a solid color and then using editing software to replace the solid color with another image.

Chroma key technology has only been around for a few decades but has already changed the face of filmmaking. It

has become an integral part of television and film production regardless of the genre. Watch any "making of" special and you will see green screens being used in a variety of situations. One example is your local weather forecast, where the weatherman stands in front of a large green screen that is keyed out and replaced with a weather map.

Green Screen

- Make sure no one appearing in your video is wearing green (or blue if you're using a blue screen).

- Also avoid green (or blue) props and other objects.

- Experiment with different clothing colors. Dark-colored clothes may create

more of a green rim around foreground objects than light colors.

- Some software packages provide dedicated green and blue screen effects, which may require the screen to be a specific color. If these effects don't work, use the chroma key effect.

Keying in Backgrounds

- The background you key in can be as simple as a solid color or as complex as a virtual studio.

- There are sites where you can download or purchase slick-looking video backing tracks, which you

can loop to form a digital background.

- Experiment with different pictures, colors, animations, and video clips to find the background that works best for your video.

Once you record your green screen footage, you can remove the green parts of the image and replace it with your own background. The chroma key tool in your editing software will allow you to remove or "key out" every instance of a certain color in the video image. Unless your subject and background were perfectly lit during filming, you will have to adjust the parameters of the chroma key to get the best result possible.

Evenly Lit

- For a green screen image to work, the green (or blue) background must be lit as evenly as possible.

- The best way to do this is to light your subject and green screen separately.

- Your subject should stand six to twelve feet from the background so that his shadow does not spill onto it.

- Typically two or more lights are used to light the green screen, but you may be able to light it with only one.

Green Screen Paint

- Many professionals will tell you that the screen color must be just the right shade of green, or that the screen must be made of certain material.

- Some materials and colors do work better than others, but in reality you can make an effective green screen from just about any smooth, green surface.

- You can buy specific material made especially for green screens, use a solid green fabric, or simply paint a wall or piece of wood a solid green color.

STOP MOTION

Stop motion is time consuming and tedious, but it can produce amazing-looking animations

Stop motion is an animation technique that makes static objects appear to be moving. When our eyes see two or more static images in quick succession, we perceive the sequence of frames as a continuous moving picture.

Stop motion was one of the first special effects techniques ever invented. It was used in the 1898 film *The Humpty Dumpty*

Circus to make a toy circus come to life. Other notable films that make extensive use of stop motion include *King Kong,* the *Star Wars* trilogy, and *The Nightmare Before Christmas.*

Object manipulation is the earliest form of stop motion animation. To manipulate, photograph an object, move it a tiny bit, and then photograph it again. Although this is very time

Importance of a Tripod

- It is very important to support the camera so it does not shake as you take the photos. A shaky camera will make your stop motion appear chaotic and lack continuity.

- Be sure not to accidentally change the exposure or

focus of the camera during the shooting of a scene.

- You can move the camera and the object together, or only move the camera and keep the object stationary to achieve different camera moves, such as panning and dollying.

Stop Motion Objects

- Select an object for your stop motion animation that is interesting. Some good choices are clay figures, Legos, dolls, or action figures.

- Be creative in your choice. Most of the obvious objects have been used a lot in these types of videos.

- Claymation is the generalized term for clay animation, a form of stop animation using clay.

- The show South Park started as a stop motion animated short using construction paper cutouts as characters.

consuming, it's also one of the easiest forms of stop motion. Although simple object manipulation can be easy, it can quickly become complex when you're dealing with multiple objects and trying to create distinct paths and events for each different object.

Before the advent of computer animation, traditional 2D drawn animation was stop motion. Animators would have to put down a single drawing, take a photo of it with a film camera, replace that drawing with another, take another picture, and so on.

Pixilation is a form of stop motion where real people are used instead of objects, drawings, or clay. You can make actors do seemingly impossible things with pixilation. Actors can appear to slide around the floor without walking, disappear through walls, and change clothes instantly.

Nowadays movies almost universally use CGI, which has caused stop motion animation to become an obsolete special effects tool in feature film.

However, stop motion is still being used in children's programming, commercials, music videos, and television shows.

Move Your Object

- Move your object in small increments before every shot. The amount you move the object should be consistent in every shot.

- Do not change the lighting of a scene during shooting. Natural light will fluctuate over time, so it is always better to use artificial light that you can control.

- The more photos you take, the smoother the video will look when you put it all together. Make sure your camera has plenty of memory so it can fit a lot of pictures.

Assembling Your Project

- Putting together a stop motion on your computer is similar to creating a slideshow, except instead of showing each image for a few seconds you show it only for a fraction of a second.

- Stop motion animations usually use a picture dura-tion of one to three frames-per-photo.

- At three frames-per-photo, you'll see ten photos every second.

- The timing you choose to use will affect the overall tempo and length of your film.

TEXT DESIGN
The fundamental rules of good text design should not be broken

There are many instances when you will have to use text in your video. Thoughtful text design for your film's titles, subtitles, and credits shouldn't be overlooked. You should spend as much time choosing fonts as you do choosing your transitions, graphics, and music. They contribute to the overall feel of your video just as much as any other element does.

Typefaces can be divided into two main categories: serif

and sans serif. Serif typefaces have small features at the end of strokes within letters while sans serif fonts do not. Times New Roman and Garamond are common examples of serif typefaces. Great variety exists among both serif and sans serif typefaces. Both groups contain fonts designed for setting large amounts of body text, and others intended primarily as decorative.

Title Design

- Although you can more easily read black letters on white paper, this rule does not carry over to video.

- In video, you can usually read light characters over a dark background more easily.

- White text on a black background usually works the best.

- You may be able to get away with using dark text if you already have a relatively light background.

Avoid Thin Lines

- Avoid using fonts with very thin lines in your video.

- The interlaced display of a television can cause characters with thin lines to flicker noticeably.

- This is especially true with fonts and graphics that have lines that are only one pixel thick.

- The closer these thin lines get to horizontal, the more pronounced the flickering or buzzing becomes.

While typefaces with serifs are often considered easier to read in long passages in print, sans serif tend to be easier to read in video and film. This is because the serifs can sometimes blend letters together. Script typefaces do not lend themselves to quantities of body text. They are typically used for logos or invitations.

The presence or absence of serifs is only one of many factors to consider when choosing a typeface.

Adding Depth

- A large, bold, and unique font will not always be enough to make your text jump off the background.

- Use outlines, gradients, or drop shadows to give your titles more depth.

- An outline can give your text more depth by making it appear as raised lettering.

- Drop shadows create the illusion of a title that floats just above the background.

The Right Font

- Since there are thousands of different fonts available, choosing the right one can be difficult.

- Try to pick a font that will match the subject matter of your film.

- Keep the font style consistent with the project, genre, and the mood you want to portray.

- Use common sense. An elegant script-type font may be perfect for a wedding video but will appear out of place in a skateboard video.

TITLE SEQUENCES

The title sequence sets the tone for the entire movie

Titles are often an afterthought for video makers, but they shouldn't be. A stylish opening title, even if it's only ten seconds long with your name and the name of your video clip, can do much to set the mood of the video, and when properly executed, add an immediate air of professionalism. The opposite is also true. An amateurish-looking title sequence will immediately put off your viewers.

Minimal credits are usually white titles that simply fade in and out in sequence over a black background. The soundtrack is sometimes silent. These title sequences are short, simple, and to the point and do not attract much attention to themselves. Woody Allen uses these types of title sequences in virtually all of his films.

A more common style is the narrative sequence. The film

Title Sequence

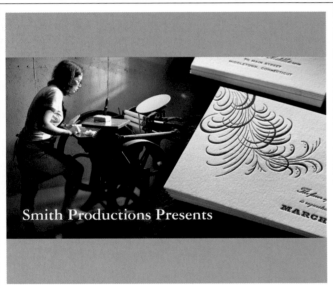

Smith Productions Presents

- Overture-style title sequences are like a self-contained show of their own. Sometimes they rely heavily on graphics and sometimes they feature montages of live action that act like previews of the film.

- Unlike narrative-style titles, overture-style titles play out completely before the story begins.

- If you create an overture opening, your backgrounds can be almost anything; abstract video, processed photos, and animation are frequently used.

Action/Title Safe

- Title and action safe guides are used to ensure that important content isn't placed outside the viewable areas of a television screen.

- Most video-editing programs will generate title and action safe margins in the preview window.

- Obeying the title and action safe boundaries is less crucial when your video will be shown only on the Internet.

- If there is any chance your video will appear on television, it is best to make sure that your title sequence fits within the safe areas.

begins immediately with the opening credits superimposed over the film playing beneath them. Title timing and placement are important in narrative-style credits, but the video piece playing behind it is even more crucial. If the material's too interesting, the audience won't notice the credits; but if it's too plain, it will look like filler. Good shots for narrative credits show things about the story's characters and situation but stay away from introducing important plot points that the audience might miss while it's reading the titles.

Some movies don't have opening titles; they just get right into the story. This technique may work for some of your videos. A title is not mandatory. The main thing to remember is that all of these titles set the mood for your work and progress the story just as every scene in your piece should do. They are not just arbitrary fonts with random colors thrown somewhere in your video. Your video should be stronger once the title is added.

Motion

- Adding motion to a title sequence will make it more dynamic and help separate it from the background.

- All editing software allows you to easily make your title zoom in and out, fly across the screen, and move in many other ways.

- Be sure not to make your title scroll too slowly, so that it flickers, or too fast, so that it is unreadable.

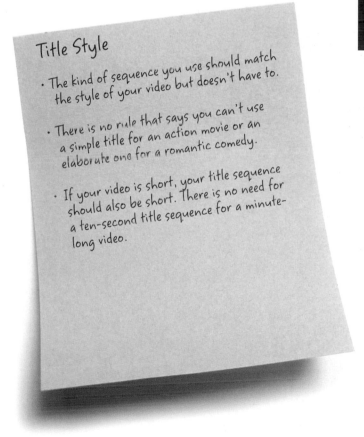

Title Style

- The kind of sequence you use should match the style of your video but doesn't have to.

- There is no rule that says you can't use a simple title for an action movie or an elaborate one for a romantic comedy.

- If your video is short, your title sequence should also be short. There is no need for a ten-second title sequence for a minute-long video.

CREDITS & SUBTITLES
Always remember to give credit where credit is due

Audiences may not pay much attention to your credits, but they are important to your cast and crew. People like to be recognized for all of the hard work they put into your film.

The closing credits usually begin with the cast in order of appearance, then a repeat of the opening names and titles, followed by staff and crew names. They are followed by the special effects credits, music, and lastly, special thanks.

Subtitles are used for films shot in a language other than the language that the audience speaks. The translation will be displayed in the lower part of the screen as the actors speak in their native language. If you shoot scenes in another language, be it Spanish or a foreign alien language, you need to add subtitles. You may also need subtitles if the dialogue of an interview subject is inaudible or distorted.

Credit Roll

- The most common way to show closing credits is to use the credit roll, where credits scroll vertically, from the bottom of the screen to the top.

- Almost all editing software lets you easily create simple scrolling text.

- The speed and duration of your credit roll will mostly depend on the length of your credits.

- Experiment with different lengths to find what works best.

Fading Credit

- An alternative to scrolling credits is to use credits that fade in and out.

- Since the eye doesn't have to track the text as it moves, fading credits are more readable than scrolling credits.

- You should keep your credits on screen long enough for them to be read aloud two to three times.

- Fading credits are often used on films with a smaller cast and crew.

The subtitles should be large enough so that they are legible on any size television. A very common style for subtitles includes a backdrop. Backdrops help to call out text on the screen and make it easier to read. The color of the backdrop should be opposite to the color of the text.

The idea of transcribing all of the lines of dialogue, typing them, and placing them in the correct position in your video can seem like a tedious time-consuming task. However, filmmakers who shoot films with a lot of subtitles can use specialized tools to make the process easier. All of the

text is written and saved in a text-based format that includes the text for each subtitle, the fonts, the style information, and, most importantly, the time codes that correspond to the starting time and duration of each text element. The file can then be imported into your editing program to create your subtitles.

Lower Third Text

- The lower third of the screen is often used to display a person's name, a song title, a person's job title, a location, etc.

- Lower third text often appears in television news productions and documentaries.

- The lower text may appear with or without an anchoring graphic underneath the text. This graphic may be stationary or animated.

- Your lower third text and/ or graphic should be consistent in style and form throughout your video.

Subtitles

- Videos intended for an international audience or films with dialogue in more than one language must have subtitles.

- Captions are different from subtitles in that they are intended for deaf and hard-of-hearing audiences.

- Subtitles should appear exactly when, or just slightly before the person on screen starts to talk.

- Subtitles can be created the same way you create regular titles, the only difference being their size and positioning.

ANIMATION

Even if you have no artistic ability, you can still make animated videos

Looking for that extra something to make your videos really shine? Why not try a little animation? The idea of animation can be a little intimidating, but computer animation has never been so available to the average video maker.

Most video editing applications let you create simple titles and glide them across the screen, but you can also animate other elements, such as photos and graphics. These programs can make the computer do the most tedious parts of animation. All you need to do is set certain "key" frames in the animation, and the program figures out all the frames in between. This is called "tweening," and it is the most labor-saving invention in all of animation history.

Graphics to Avoid

Take the Subway to the Game!

- TV and video streaming outputs are at a much lower resolution than that of computer monitors.

- Avoid using graphics with a lot of small detail. You will lose some of this detail due to the lower resolution of the video output.

- Stay away from saturated or bright colors, such as reds, yellows, true whites, magentas, and yellow-greens, as they tend to create a bleeding or halo effect.

Charts and Graphs

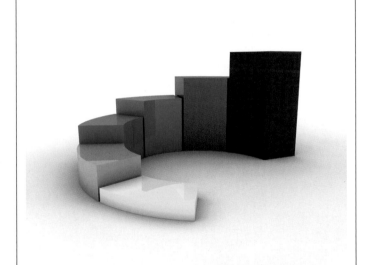

- As useful as pie charts and bar graphs can be in print media, they can be even more effective when used in your video.

- You can add animation to the values of a graph or chart to create a lively effect.

- Be careful; charts full of data such as Excel spreadsheets usually look bad once they've been encoded, compressed, and streamed.

To make a graphic fly across the screen, for example, you would set its location for Frame 1, add a key frame, and then set its new location in Frame 50 with a key frame. The program will then create smooth movement between the two key frames. You can also easily use key frames to tween many other elements. Draw a face in Frame 1, then drag up the corners of the mouth in Frame 30, and you've made a smoothly tweened smile with just a couple of mouse clicks. Once you know the process you will find many ways to use key frames and tweening.

It's important to regulate how fast you move from one key frame to another. Key frames spaced closely together will make an object move fast, and key frames spaced far apart will make the object move slowly. A good animation program will give you control over these dynamics.

Once you learn how to use these tools to give your titles and graphics motion and animation, you can harness a whole new set of skills to help tell your story.

Key Frames

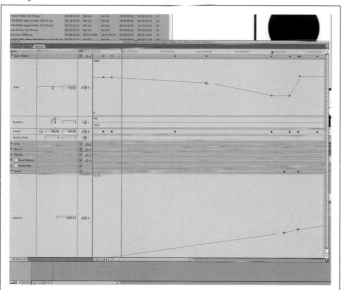

- Virtually any aspect of your video that can be altered during editing can be key framed, which will make those values change over time.

- The key frame is both extremely simple and extremely complicated at the same time. As simple as it is to do, key framing is considered an advanced technique.

- Not all video editing software will let you do key framing.

Bitmap versus Vector

- Computer graphics fall into two broad categories: bitmap and vector.

- Bitmap graphics, which are also sometimes called raster images, control pixels individually. They are used to produce detailed images such as photographs.

- Vector graphics control groups of pixels together using mathematical calculations called vectors.

- These are often used to create images containing illustrations and text.

- Vector images can be scaled with no loss in quality, while bitmap graphics can become pixilated when scaled beyond 100 percent.

3D GRAPHICS & CGI

If you have the time and perseverance, you can build complex characters and worlds

CGI (computer-generated images) is used for visual effects because computer-generated effects are more controllable than other more physically-based effects. CGI allows the creation of images that would not be feasible using any other technology. The recent availability of CGI software and increased computer speeds have allowed anybody with

enough time and dedication to produce the same effects seen in professional-grade films.

3D computer graphics are often referred to as 3D models. The process of creating 3D computer graphics can be sequentially divided into three basic phases: 3D modeling, which describes the process of forming the shape of an

Computer-generated Animation

- *Toy Story* was the first full-length completely computer-generated animated film.

- For the movie, Pixar created a network of computers to handle the task of "render-

  ing" each of the 114,000 frames in the seventy-seven minute movie.

- Using one single-processor computer to render *Toy Story* would have taken forty-three years.

Particle Systems

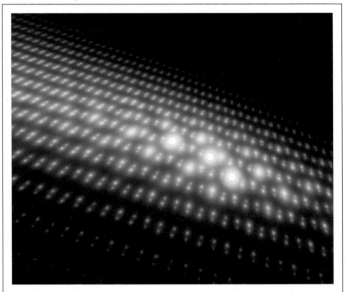

- Particle systems are one of the most popular motion graphics tools and are responsible for producing multiple animated elements.

- Particles are points in 3D space that can be represented by a wide variety of stationary or animated objects.

- Particles can be emitted in small numbers or in the thousands and can be in the form of a single point, a line, a grid, a plane, or an object.

- Particle systems are used to make fire, explosions, smoke, moving water, sparks, falling leaves, etc.

object; layout and animation, which describes the motion and placement of objects within a scene; and 3D rendering, which produces an image of an object.

The only limiting factor in creating 3D objects is your own determination and creativity. Working with CGI and 3D graphics is an entirely different discipline from making videos. It's up to you to really get going in this art form. Still, you might be surprised how easy it can be to add animation to your projects. Even if you aren't really an artist and have no interest in 3D modeling, you can find 3D objects and premade effects online.

3D Modeling

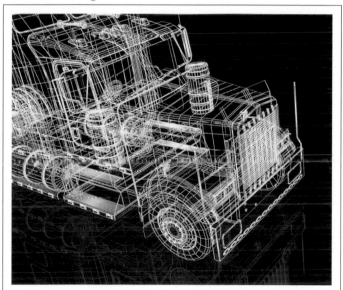

- 3D modeling is the process of developing a mathematical, wireframe representation of any three-dimensional object, either inanimate or living.

- 3D models represent a 3D object using a collection of points in 3D space, connected by various geometric entities such as triangles, lines, and curved surfaces.

- 3D rendering is the 3D computer graphics process of automatically converting 3D wireframe models into 2D images with 3D photorealistic effects on a computer.

Machinima

- Machinima is the use of real-time 3D graphics rendering engines to generate computer animation.

- Machinima video makers often use graphic engines from video games to make their films.

- Making a computer-animated film requires hours to render a single frame of animation, but in machinima, it is instantaneous.

- Sims 2, Quake, Halo, Second Life, and World of Warcraft are some of the most popular game engines used in machinima.

GRAPHIC PROGRAMS
Use these programs to do animation and graphics work

Before computers were widely available, motion graphics were costly and time-consuming, limiting their use to only high budget film and TV projects. Just as nonlinear editors and affordable cameras made it possible for the consumer to shoot and edit video, applications like Adobe After Effects and AutoDesk Maya bring the power of a full visual effects studio to your desktop computer. All that's required from the average videographer is time, patience, and practice.

There are two basic types of motion graphics software. The first category includes video manipulation packages like Adobe After Effects or AutoDesk's Combustion. These programs are used for many things, including enhancing existing videos, creating title sequences, and compositing different elements into a shot.

Adobe After Effects

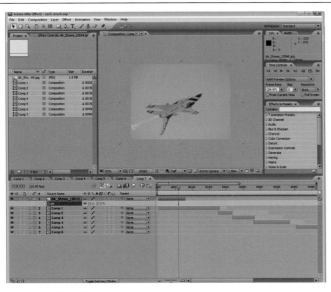

- Adobe After Effects is one of the most recognized motion graphics applications available.

- After Effects is primarily used for creating motion graphics and visual effects.

- After Effects allows users to animate, alter, and com-

- posite media in 2D and 3D space with various built-in tools and third party plug-ins.

- If you are familiar with Adobe Photoshop, or Premiere, the After Effects interface will be easy to learn.

Apple Motion

- Apple Motion is a software application produced by Apple.

- It is used to create and edit motion graphics, for titling, and for 2D and 3D compositing for visual effects.

- Motion is very similar in some ways to Adobe After Effects.

- Motion is included as part of the Final Cut Studio suite.

The second category of software includes 3D modeling and animation applications like LightWave or Maya. Animators use them to model, texture, animate, and finally render out elements for a shot. Whether it's a virtual studio or an angry monster, these tools can create anything the user wants.

The two types of software packages enhance each other. Many motion graphics animators learn several graphics packages. Although many trends in motion graphics are based on specific software's capabilities, the software is only a tool the designer uses while bringing the vision to life.

Adobe Photoshop

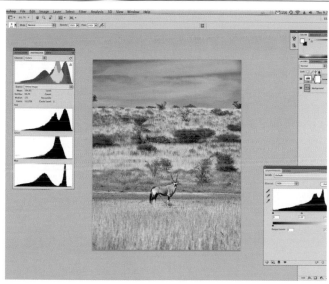

- Adobe Photoshop is the industry standard image editing program for professional raster graphics and other digital art graphics.

- It can be used to touch up photos and create titles and graphics.

- Photoshop has strong ties with other Adobe software for media editing, animation, and authoring.

- A very popular technique for video, Adobe Photoshop makes still photographs come alive on screen by showing a foreground subject moving against a static background.

Learning

- Many motion graphic programs can be quite difficult to learn.

- Some people are able to teach themselves these programs simply by opening up the program and exploring all the options the program has.

- If you really want to learn the ins and outs of these programs though, you should consider purchasing a book or taking a class on the specific program you want to learn.

- There are many great video tutorials online made by regular users that can teach you anything you want to know.

203

SCREENING
Get your film seen by a larger audience

Finally, your movie is finished. However, don't think that the finishing of your film means that your work is done. In fact, the hardest part lies ahead: getting your masterpiece seen by an audience.

One way to get your film seen by a larger audience is to hold a screening. An advanced movie screening is a promotional event as well as a way to get the public to see your movie.

The logical place to hold your screening would seem to be a movie theater. This is a great idea, especially if you feel you can fill the seats and sell enough tickets to cover the rental cost. Look ahead at least eight weeks to schedule your event for sufficient planning and outreach.

Avoid holidays and local planned events when you pick a screening date to avoid competition. Picking a centrally

Pre-screening

- Before you try to show your film to a larger audience, it is a good idea to gather your friends and family for a prescreening.

- Ask for feedback and take note of jokes that fall flat, plot points that people miss, and other things that you may have to change.

- You'd be surprised how much you can get a feel for how a film resonates with an audience simply by watching it with them.

- This is your movie, though; don't let a few comments change your entire vision.

Theater Screening

- Besides getting unbiased feedback from strangers, screening your film also provides the opportunity to draw in other filmmakers and do some networking.

- Bring evaluation forms and pens to hand out as people

file in. The information you collect can go a long way in helping to attract distributors and aid in advertising.

- If you plan to have Q&A afterward, make sure there is a working microphone available.

located theater will make it easier for your audience to come to your screening. Invite a mixed audience of filmmakers, your target audience for the film, and everyone else you know.

Other places make fine advanced screening venues, as well. Many apartment complexes have big screening rooms on site nowadays and they are often inexpensive to rent for a night.

Equipment for Screening

- Write out everything you will need for your event, from the type of equipment you have to bring to how many volunteers you'll need.

- Playhouses are also good screening spaces but may require you to bring a large TV or digital projector, as not all will have their own.

- The larger the screen, the more impact your film will have on the audience.

Get the Word Out

- Do anything you can to get the word out about your screening; the more people who show up, the better.

- Distribute flyers, use e-mail announcements, contact local media, and post an ad on craigslist.com and filmmaking Web sites.

- Make an event on Facebook or Myspace and invite everybody in your social network.

- Most communities have free newspapers where you can place ads for an event. Their rates are usually very affordable.

FILM FESTIVALS

There are hundreds of film festivals around the country that you can submit your film to

Getting your film into a festival is like any other career achievement. It's something to enjoy, something to put on your resume, and an opportunity to gain some exposure and make some connections. It's very rarely, however, a giant breakthrough that results in funding for a major production. There are hundreds of film festivals in the United States, with thousands of filmmakers screening their work every year; yet, when you see commercials for upcoming Hollywood releases, almost none of them were directed by filmmakers who just got discovered at a festival.

Experienced festival filmmakers suggest that you should know what you want your submission to achieve before you

The Festival Circuit

- Nearly ten thousand films are submitted to the Sundance Film Festival every year, and of those, fewer than one hundred are accepted.

- At a smaller film festival you may only see twenty or thirty people at the screening, and most of them will be other filmmakers and their friends and family.

- Sometimes film festivals focus on a specific genre or subject matter.

- Most film festivals require filmmakers to pay an entry fee to have their works considered for screening.

Online Festivals

- In 2005, the world's first online film festival was created, the GreenCine Online Film Festival. Since then, there have been thousands more online film festivals.

- Online fests are great because they allow filmmakers from around the world to showcase their work in front of a global audience.

- Be careful, though: If you show your film in one of these online fests you greatly diminish that film's chances of getting into mainstream film festivals.

submit it. Is it to get you an agent or a publicist? Is it to make enough of an impact to get invited to other festivals? Is it to attract investors to fund your next project? Knowing what you want out of the experience will help you achieve it.

Filmmakers make films for an audience, and that's where a film festival comes in. Unless you rented a theater for a screening, a film festival is usually your first chance to show your film to complete strangers who have nothing invested in your film. This means that a festival is probably your first opportunity to get an honest reaction to your work.

Withoutabox.com is a Web site–based film submission service; it is a division of the IMDb (Internet Movie Database). The Web site offers filmmakers a platform to submit their films to over three thousand film festivals around the world. Some film festivals won't accept direct submissions anymore and prefer that you go through an online festival submission service.

DVD Title

- If your DVD art doesn't look professional, send your film without any. As long as you write legibly, don't worry about a hand-labeled disc hurting your chances of acceptance.

- A LightScribe-enabled DVD burner and DVD discs with LightScribe coating will allow you to create printed disc surfaces without the use of ink or a printer.

- Printed DVDs produce the best-looking DVDs, but the inkjet cartridges can be expensive.

- Avoid using paper sticker labels on your DVDs.

Length

- Length is the number one item judges take into consideration when deciding which films will be screened at their festival.

- The shorter the better; no film can be too brief.

- While a thirty-minute film is still considered a short, it will have a tougher time getting into festivals than a twelve-minute film.

- Film festivals want to screen as many short films as possible. It will mean more filmmakers in attendance and more film Web sites linking to the festival's Web site.

ONLINE DISTRIBUTION

Online distribution is an easy way to get a lot of people to see your work

The online potential for movie marketing became clear as soon as user-created content exploded on YouTube and MySpace. Hollywood will continue to spend big money on marketing its new movies, but entrepreneurial do-it-yourself moviemakers do the same thing using the Internet and spending a lot less money.

Traditionally, there have been two ways for online film companies to make money off independent films: Charge a rental fee to view an entire film or run ads against films that are offered for free. However, data suggests that few consumers seem willing to pay a rental fee for an independent film when there is so much free content available on the Internet and

Streaming Video

- Many distribution companies and film festivals will refuse to deal with any producer who makes his film available on YouTube.

- To them, the very act of being on YouTube is seen as spoiling the film for any other form of distribution.

- For this reason, it may be a smart idea to exhaust all other possible forms of distribution before uploading your video to YouTube or other streaming video sites like it.

iTunes

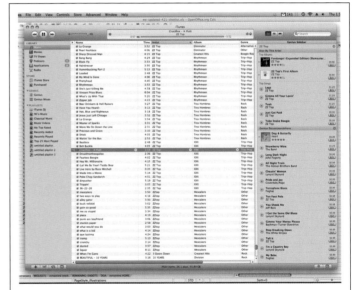

- Getting your film on iTunes will involve using an aggregate company since Apple will not deal with indie filmmakers directly.

- Content aggregators deal with short films or feature films. Rarely does a single aggregator deal in both forms of films.

- In a more perfect world of independent film distribution, iTunes would allow all feature filmmakers to upload their work; hopefully this will happen in the future.

television. Ad rates are driven lower and lower by an endless supply of bad video that is uploaded to the Internet daily.

If you are mulling online distribution, remember that it's anyone's guess right now if you will make any money. However, right now the Internet can help you create buzz around your film, and buzz is what you want. Buzz could attract consumers who are willing to spend money to watch your movie or an investor who discovers your film online and decides to help you get your next film made.

Downloadable Movies

- Peer-to-peer (p2p) file sharing options like BitTorrent offer a great way to get your content to the masses.

- Allowing your film to be downloaded for free sounds like a foolish idea, but some filmmakers have had success distributing their film this way.

- The independent movie *Ink* was downloaded via BitTorrent 400,000 times in a single week and exposed the film to a large audience, leading to higher DVD and Blu-Ray sales in return.

Web Site Promotion

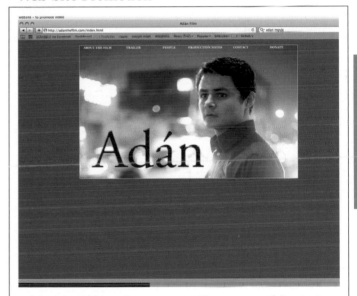

- It is a good idea to have a Web site to help promote your movie.

- This doesn't have to be a state-of-the-art masterpiece. A MySpace, Facebook, or Blogger page will work just fine.

- The purpose of the site is to host your trailer or clips, your press images, your reviews, and to give people interested in your film an easy way to contact you.

FINISHING

GETTING RIGHTS

Don't include anything in your video that you don't have the right to use

If you are interested in posting your movie online, distributing it on DVD, or just generally sharing it with the world, you need to be certain that you own the copyright to everything contained in the movie. If you expect your movie ever to be viewed by a wide audience, getting rights can help you avoid any legal problems with the content.

Anyone who speaks on camera, or whose name you use, should sign a release giving you permission to use his image. Taking care of business beforehand can eliminate headaches afterwards when dealing with copyright, permissions, and talent releases.

Secure permission to shoot in private locations by getting

Signing a Release

- You must get a signed release form for anyone who is identifiable in your video.

- You can use a simple agreement to protect yourself from invasion-of-privacy lawsuits brought by your actors or even bystanders in your video productions.

- By signing the release, the person waives the right of privacy and cannot sue you at a later date for copying or exhibiting the tape.

- If your actor is under age, have his or her guardian sign instead.

Release Form

- Doing an Internet search for "talent releases" will bring up a host of links ranging from affordable contract packages to basic free agreements that you can alter to fit your needs.

- If you would rather make your own release form, make sure you include a

- place for the performer's signature, the date, and the rights your performer is giving up or waiving.

- If the performer doesn't sign the release in your presence, be sure to ask him to have his signature notarized.

the signature of the location's owner. Although billboards and storefronts appear in public places and you can shoot them legally, it might be a good idea to ask the advertisers and store owners for their permissions, as well. If you're sure they'll give you permission, you could ask for it just for the sake of good will or for the product placement opportunities it may bring about.

Ordinarily, it is legal to shoot in public places without anyone's permission. However, if you plan to shoot in a congested area where the presence of yourself and your gear may obstruct pedestrian or automobile traffic, talk with your police department. Ask whether you need a shooting permit.

Secure permission to use music, photographs, or other copyrighted materials. The owners of the works must sign the forms.

Video directors should be careful to obtain copyright and various other permissions when creating their productions. Creating a checklist of permissions to secure will help keep the ship righted and the production out of court.

Getting an Attorney

- When in doubt about your rights or obligations, consult a lawyer. Lawyers for a film project are definitely not all the same. Just because someone's uncle does probate law does not mean that he is qualified to do entertainment law.

- Attorneys who specialize in the field of intellectual property are usually listed under "Patent Attorneys" in the phone book.

- Some people might claim that any release that wasn't prepared by a lawyer is not legally binding, so it's best to have a lawyer look over your release.

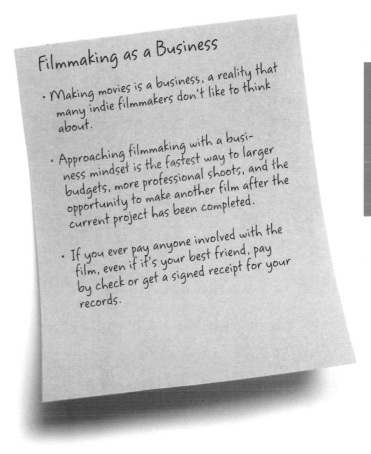

Filmmaking as a Business

- Making movies is a business, a reality that many indie filmmakers don't like to think about.

- Approaching filmmaking with a business mindset is the fastest way to larger budgets, more professional shoots, and the opportunity to make another film after the current project has been completed.

- If you ever pay anyone involved with the film, even if it's your best friend, pay by check or get a signed receipt for your records.

CONTESTS

Compete with other filmmakers at film contests held online and around the country

You don't have to be a professional to win money from online video contests. All you need is a good idea, creativity, and some basic equipment and software. There are online video contests geared toward all skill levels, and they're a great place to showcase your video talents.

If you've been itching to get your video out there and you don't mind adhering to a contest's restrictions, then check out the array of video contests online. Whatever your long-term goals for your video production are, you can get some good exposure and meet new people.

Winning a video contest can also improve your resume and score you some valuable prizes, but first you have to

Online Contests

- At any given time, there are dozens of online film contests being held.

- Most contests on the Web are designed to promote a particular product or service.

- These promotional product video contests frequently have bigger prizes since they're fueled by marketing strategies.

- Sometimes, the winning video may be used as the basis of a future commercial for the product or the video itself may be used as a commercial.

Prizes

- Prizes often include prize money, vacations, trips to film festivals, gift cards, and celebrity meetings.

- Most contests let you submit more than one entry. The more entries you submit, the better chance you have of winning a prize.

- Many film contests are free, while others charge a small admission fee.

- Participating in an online film contest teaches you a lot about producing commercials for clients and can result in video to use in your reel.

make sure that your tape gets the proper exposure it needs and that it is put together in a way that will catch the eye of the judges.

Make sure that your video is appropriate for the contests you enter. If entering a specific contest is the long-term goal for you, be sure to create a video tailored specifically for the contest's needs. Whatever route you go, be sure that your content is original, rather than regurgitated material from previous films.

Read the Fine Print

- Before you submit your film to a contest, read all the contest rules carefully.

- Fill out your entry forms legibly. If judges can't read your entry form, they may not give you a chance.

- Do not send a contest submission on an unspecified format. If you only have a DVD, and the contest rules request a VHS, then it's your responsibility to convert it.

- Remember, a contest may receive thousands of submissions, so don't give the judges any reason to dump your film by the wayside.

Keep Your Head Up

- Despite your best efforts, you may not win an award.

- There is simply no way to know how a judge will react to a given movie in advance.

- The fact that the number of judges is often fairly small can result in unpredictable results.

- Generally, judges love a quick opening, precise editing, good pacing, an obvious conclusion, and, above all, a good story.

DISTRIBUTION
Strategies for getting your film into the right hands

Hollywood studios have retained strong control over the distribution of films, both their own mainstream films and those made by independent producers. As things stand today, a filmmaker needs to find a distributor in order to reach anyone outside of the festival circuit. Only distributors have the relationships with exhibitors, cable companies, DVD rental services, and stores. Most films reach the world audience through these studios and a handful of distributors.

However, thanks to the great Internet, it's become much easier for indie filmmakers to find audiences and eventually buyers for their products. Self-distribution is an increasingly enticing option. You likely wrote, directed, and edited your film, so why not take it upon yourself to get it in front of audiences, too?

Trailers

THE FOLLOWING **PREVIEW** HAS BEEN APPROVED FOR
APPROPRIATE AUDIENCES
BY THE MOTION PICTURE ASSOCIATION OF AMERICA, INC.

www.filmratings.com   www.mpaa.org

- A trailer can be one of the best ways to market your film.

- Select clips that identify the main characters and conflicts. Also choose shorter clips that identify some of the more dramatic or comedic moments of the primary action.

- Typically, the majority of the trailer is taken from the first act of the film, and then the rest is a collage of the middle acts.

- Conventionally, a short film trailer should not go over thirty seconds and a feature should be around a minute and a half.

Business Cards

ERIC WESTPHELING
STILL & MOTION PICTURE PHOTOGRAPHY
WWW.ERICWESTPHELING.COM
917.584.6153

- Business cards are an old school, but still effective, way of letting people know about your talents. Be sure to include your company name, Web site address, your name, title, phone, and e-mail address.

- Design a creative and attractive card. While a simple design works well for an attorney or businessman, a filmmaker should have a more eye-catching card, but one where the information still reads clearly and quickly.

- There are many online sites that can inexpensively print hundreds of cards.

Self-promotion and advertising are important for the independent film more so than studio productions because independents do not have the same level of marketing resources that big studios do. The independent filmmaker needs to be extra creative with getting the word out.

A press release is the cheapest and easiest way to start the promotional campaign for your film. A press release is a one-page synopsis of your movie that will be distributed to the public. Newspapers, magazines, and broadcasters receive hundreds of press releases daily. To get noticed, be sure you create a proper release, send it to the right person, and, at the same time, make it stand apart from all the others. Create a media kit that can be downloaded off your Web site. Kits typically include high-resolution stills, a poster image, a trailer, and key information about the film. This kit allows bloggers and media to easily pick up your story. The resulting attention paid to your film will build interest that may help attract traditional distributors.

Movie Posters

- People judge books by their covers, and they also judge movies by their covers. Even if your film is great, a badly designed DVD cover will turn people away from watching your movie.

- If you are bad at graphic design, find someone who can design your poster for you.

- The colors, logo, font, and art used for your cover should be used on your Web site, film festival postcards, and other promotional materials to create a consistent branded look.

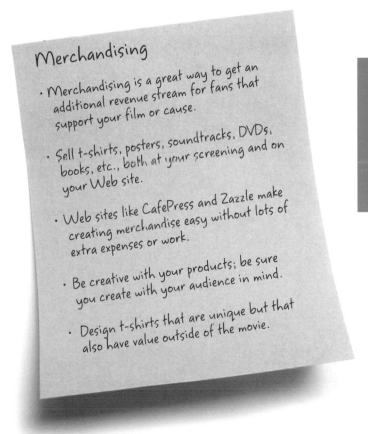

Merchandising

- Merchandising is a great way to get an additional revenue stream for fans that support your film or cause.

- Sell t-shirts, posters, soundtracks, DVDs, books, etc., both at your screening and on your Web site.

- Web sites like CafePress and Zazzle make creating merchandise easy without lots of extra expenses or work.

- Be creative with your products; be sure you create with your audience in mind.

- Design t-shirts that are unique but that also have value outside of the movie.

HISTORY

As long as there have been movies, there have been people trying to make them cheaply

Prior to the 1950s, the idea that a regular person could make a feature film from his own financial resources would have been ridiculous. Since that time, however, technological changes have made it possible for anybody to make a low-budget film independent of the major Hollywood studios.

Filmmakers who make films with little or no money are known as guerilla filmmakers. On guerilla productions, one or two or a handful of individuals gather their financial resources, possibly with small investors, seek out free or inexpensive equipment, and get cast and crew to work cheaply or for free. With their tiny budgets, these filmmakers produce their movies, often under highly difficult circumstances.

Robert Rodriguez

- Robert Rodriguez made the action western movie *El Mariachi* for $7,000. The film made him a celebrity at the Sundance Film Festival and got him a deal with Columbia Pictures.

- Robert Rodriguez partially raised the money for *El Mariachi* by volunteering in medical research studies.

- Rodriguez described his experiences making the film in his book *Rebel Without a Crew*. The book and film inspired many filmmakers to pick up cameras and make no-budget movies.

The Blair Witch Project

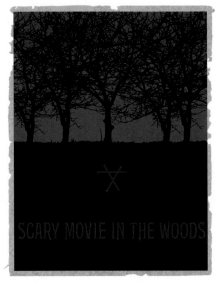

- *The Blair Witch Project* is an example of guerilla film-making at its finest.

- It was shot over six days and nights with the actors shooting all of the footage, camping out in the woods, and improvising their lines.

- One of the cameras used was bought at Circuit City and then returned for a refund after filming was completed.

- *The Blair Witch Project* holds the record for top budget: box office ratio. The film cost $22,000 to make and made $240.5 million.

Job descriptions for crew members may become a little murky in a guerilla production. With no money or status at stake, cast and crew agree to work on the film primarily to enjoy the experience or to help out friends. Without the strict regulations of unions, members of the crew may find themselves filling whatever positions are necessary for any given scene or day.

This gives the filmmakers considerably more control over the finished product, as they now must only attract a distribution company to have their film released in theaters. With the advent of the Internet, guerilla filmmakers have even more control over their product, as they can release and distribute online inexpensively and without a distribution company.

However, for every success story, there are hundreds of American guerilla films made every year that get no further than the editing room, or, at most, a couple of screenings in out-of-the-way film festivals.

Spike Lee

- Spike Lee's first feature-length film, *She's Gotta Have It,* was made on a guerilla budget of $175,000 and made $7,137,502 at the box office.

- Because the film's budget was so tight, there were no retakes of any scenes.

- Spike Lee told the cast not to throw away any aluminum cans when they broke for lunch so he could turn them in for recycling money.

- Spike describes the making of the movie in his book *Spike Lee's Gotta Have It: Inside Guerrilla Filmmaking.*

Kevin Smith

- Kevin Smith's first film, *Clerks,* was financed largely by credit cards and money borrowed from family and friends.

- *Clerks* was filmed at the same store in which director Kevin Smith was working at the time.

- *Clerks* went on to win several awards, jump starting a Hollywood career for Smith and proving to a generation of filmmakers that hard work and dedication make up for a lack of big budget and experience.

MOTIVATION

When you have your heart set on making a movie, nothing can stop you

Perhaps the greatest thing about guerilla filmmaking is that there are no rules. You can make whatever you want. However, this is also one bad thing about guerilla filmmaking. Without the pressure of an investor or a strict schedule, it is easy to go on forever without ever starting or finishing your movie. Guerilla filmmakers must be extra dedicated and committed to the story they want to tell.

The number one thing you need is passion. You need the drive and desire to know that nothing is going to get in your way. No matter what happens, you can handle it. If you have the passion, then guerilla filmmaking can be a lot of fun. There will be stresses involved in filmmaking, whether you

Shooting in the Street

- Small camcorders can be invaluable for times when you want to shoot in the field without being noticed.

- You can often record something without anybody noticing if you hold your camcorder at your side.

- If your camcorder has a red recording light on the front, see if there is an option to turn it off or place a small piece of electric tape over it.

Carrying Your Equipment

- Wear clothes that allow you to carry a lot of equipment and accessories.

- A good pair of cargo shorts with a lot of pockets can hold extra batteries, lenses, wires, tape, tools, notebooks, etc.

- Consider buying a hunter's-style vest with a lot of pockets to hold even more equipment. You may look funny wearing clothes with a few dozen pockets packed to the brim, but it can be very helpful when shooting in the field.

have no budget or a $50 million budget. Sure, they may be completely different kinds of stresses, but they will still be there. If you want to be a filmmaker, if you love movies, stop making excuses for yourself and just do it.

In the past, filmmakers had to spend years searching for financing. Guerilla filmmakers today can devote that time to improving the script, rehearsing the actors, and shooting the best possible movie. When the film is finished, guerilla filmmakers can then decide if it is good enough to launch their careers. If not they can make another feature for a few thousand dollars and try to learn from their mistakes. Digital video allows filmmakers to take greater creative risks. Given the cost of production, there is little to lose by experimenting, and a lot to gain if you can make a truly original film. Digital video and the Internet is shifting power from financiers to filmmakers, who no longer need their money, permission, or approval to make their films.

Equipment Organization

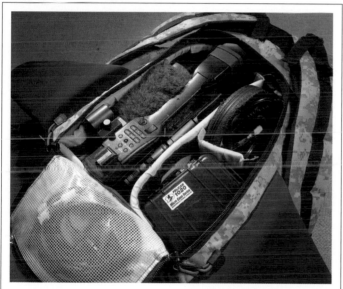

- Before you go on a shoot, lay out all of your equipment on the floor and take note of what you have.

- Write down a list of all the equipment you have and what equipment you still need.

- Organize your equipment and accessories neatly in your camera bag or on your person so you don't waste valuable time searching for them while shooting.

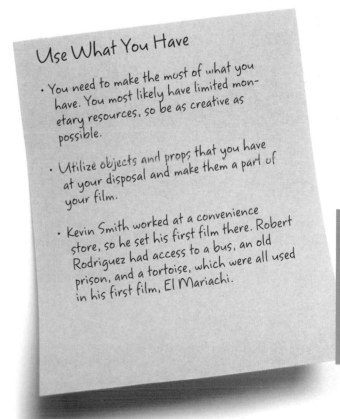

Use What You Have

- You need to make the most of what you have. You most likely have limited monetary resources, so be as creative as possible.

- Utilize objects and props that you have at your disposal and make them a part of your film.

- Kevin Smith worked at a convenience store, so he set his first film there. Robert Rodriguez had access to a bus, an old prison, and a tortoise, which were all used in his first film, El Mariachi.

CUTTING YOUR BUDGET
Strategies to cut your budget down to nothing

Think of guerilla filmmaking as more of a hobby or a way of life than a way to make money. If you approach your project with the attitude that you are doing it for the sheer love of it, you'll find that you won't feel like you've wasted your time and money producing videos.

Some filmmakers will disagree with this, but on a guerilla production, sometimes there is such a thing as too much planning. When dealing with a cast and crew who work for low or no pay, it's important to get in and get out as quickly as possible. Some people will lose interest and others may find real paying jobs if you take too long. When shooting on an ultra-low budget, you could spend months preparing and still run into a lot of problems.

If you want to make sure your low-budget film runs

Cutting Location Fees

- Location fees can easily drain a film's budget, but since you don't have a budget, this won't apply to you.

- If you only need to shoot a quick scene, you may be able to briefly shoot it at a location before anybody notices.

- If your film needs a specific indoor location, ask friends, parents, friends of friends, parents of friends, etc., for location ideas or loans.

- Offer to give the owner of the location credit on the film for allowing you to shoot there. Invite him to watch you film.

Creating a Schedule

- Devising an accurate schedule before you start your project is key to keeping it under budget. You need to know what to shoot where, and when.

- Since your cast and crew are not being paid, the shorter your schedule is the more likely people will

- be willing to work with you for free.

- In order to shoot your film in the optimal time, you need to have a very clear and intimate knowledge of your film. You need to know it shot-for-shot, angle-for-angle, and word-for-word.

smoothly and quickly, then choose an actor who is excited about the project rather than one with more experience looking for a paycheck.

Someone with less experience but who is truly in love with the project itself will work harder and give more of himself than an uninterested, more experienced person. You're asking people to work for little or no money, for long hours, and over an extended period. If you want them to stick around and give their all in spite of grueling circumstances, then you want people with a huge amount of enthusiasm.

Try to eliminate as many small parts as you can while still keeping your story intact. Have your actors use costume pieces from their own wardrobes. Most of the time you don't need to buy or make expensive costumes. Simply use pieces from the actors' own closets to cut down your clothing expenses.

Garage Sale

- Search around garage sales to find various pieces that you can use in your film.

- Garage sales are a great place to find good photographic tripods that can be used for independent filmmaking.

- Conversely, having a garage sale to sell things you don't need any more can be a great way to raise a few bucks for your project.

Beg for Money

- Be creative in coming up with ways you can raise money. Don't be embarrassed to ask for money from your friends, family, and acquaintances, but with the understanding that you'll pay them back.

- Put on special events and parties, and invite people

who are interested in your film's subject or theme.

- Donations don't always have to come in the form of cash. You can save a lot on your bottom line if you can acquire goods and services from businesses willing to donate.

PRE-PRODUCTION TIPS

Pre-production for guerilla films is all about planning a film that is within your means

Before starting work on a project, it's important to know the purpose of the film at the very start. Are you going to make a movie for art's sake or to learn the process of making a no-budget film? Or maybe you are looking to create a commercially viable movie that can be sold and generate you a profit? If you're in it strictly for the money and fame, however,

then you're probably not a guerilla filmmaker. Filmmaking this way can set you up for disappointment if you walk into it believing that you're a great filmmaker who will make all your money back.

The script is essentially the most important piece of no-budget filmmaking. It is the blueprint for your film. If the

eBay

- Good, used equipment is always better than cheap, new equipment.

- If you know exactly what you want, you can get the best deals by keeping an eye on eBay and bidding wisely.

- Besides eBay, check out the used department of electronics stores.

- You can also find other things you need for your project, like equipment, props, and costumes.

Food on Set

- Buying food is one of the things that you must spend money on during production of a guerilla film. In fact, it might be one of your largest expenses.

- A volunteer crew will not work happily or productively without nourishment.

- You don't need to provide a four-course meal. Keep it simple: Stick to easy-to-prepare, cost-effective, healthy, and hot meals that will do a good job of refueling the cast and crew.

blueprint is not designed properly, your film will fall to pieces. Every good movie is produced around a well-written script. It doesn't matter how big the budget is, how good the actors are, how incredible the explosions are, or how dynamic the visual effects are: Unless the story is moving, engaging, and believable, the film won't work.

All successful ultra low-budget filmmakers understand that you must make your film within the limits of the resources available. Start with a no-nonsense resource assessment. Determine as realistically as possible which resources, such as cash, equipment, crew, and post-production facilities, you have access to, then write your script within the framework of these resources.

Whatever kind of money you invest to make your film, the investment will be major. A couple of thousand dollars to a studio is nothing, but to the average person it is a major commitment. You have to know that no matter what comes up, no matter what happens, you will keep pressing through.

Stock Video

- If you need a shot of something but don't have the means to shoot it yourself, consider buying some stock footage.

- There are plenty of libraries of clips online that have stock footage of nearly anything and everything.

- Free stock video can also be found.

- Stock video of explosions and other effects can be keyed into your video later to increase its production value.

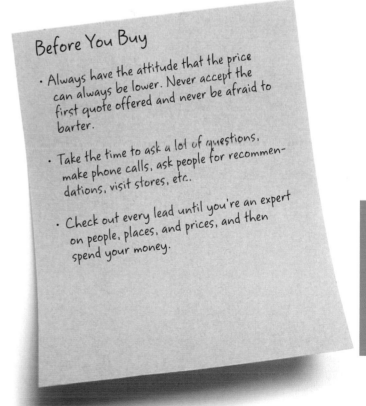

Before You Buy

- Always have the attitude that the price can always be lower. Never accept the first quote offered and never be afraid to barter.

- Take the time to ask a lot of questions, make phone calls, ask people for recommendations, visit stores, etc.

- Check out every lead until you're an expert on people, places, and prices, and then spend your money.

PRODUCTION TIPS

Now more than ever, it's possible for one person to capture great video

Filmmakers are everywhere, not just in Hollywood, and it goes without saying that the vast majority of filmmakers don't work with anything like the budget that Hollywood studios have. So can quality films be made for little or even no money? Of course they can. Is it possible for no-budget films to look cheap? Absolutely, and this is something you

need to look out for. Making it look like you had money to spend is a skill you will develop as you make more movies.

You can go out and tell any story for $10, for the cost of a DV tape. If you want to, you can go in your backyard with your camera and reshoot *Independence Day*. Anybody can do that. You'll use a fake alien ship and imitate Will Smith's voice

Get In. Get Out.

- When you shoot in a location without the proper permits or permission, you must work as quickly as possible.

- Don't waste time setting up your shots perfectly or shooting multiple takes.

- Keep your crew as small as possible so you do not draw too much attention to yourselves.

- Use personal discretion. You may be able to take longer to shoot in the middle of a park than you can on the steps of city hall.

Trouble with the Law

- If you get stopped by a police officer while filming, be as polite as possible and leave immediately.

- It is rare that a cop will ticket you unless you cause a huge disturbance.

- Most cops will simply give you a warning, make you leave the location immediately, and make you promise not to come back without the proper permits.

and have a little movie that you made for next to nothing. The thing you need to ask yourself, however, is this: "Where do I cross the line into making a low budget movie just for the sake of making a movie and risk completely destroying the story?"

A lot of low budget films seem to do that, and that's why few of them ever get sold. You have to do everything you can to make a great film. Set the bar high. Be brutally honest with yourself up front about your efforts, and which ones are wasted and which ones are worth it.

With that said, though, don't let a lack of financing curb your desire to make films. Make tons of shorts, or other types of videos. You'll learn something every time. Try different things to keep growing as a filmmaker and enrich your experiences. You'll never stop learning, and you'll never stop having fun.

Film Vehicle

- Guerilla filmmaking takes a lot of planning and a lot of tricks. You should scout all of your locations and see exactly what types of obstacles you might be faced with during filming.

- Make sure your vehicle is parked close enough to your location to set up a base.

- Wait in the vehicle until the safest time to film your scene so you cause minimal disturbance and don't run into trouble with security.

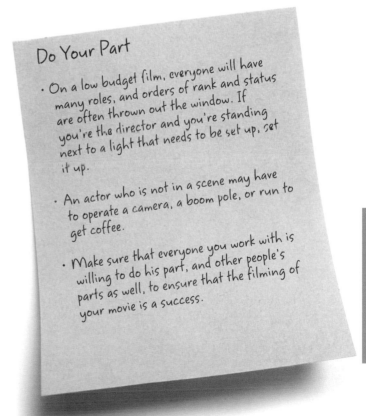

Do Your Part

- On a low budget film, everyone will have many roles, and orders of rank and status are often thrown out the window. If you're the director and you're standing next to a light that needs to be set up, set it up.

- An actor who is not in a scene may have to operate a camera, a boom pole, or run to get coffee.

- Make sure that everyone you work with is willing to do his part, and other people's parts as well, to ensure that the filming of your movie is a success.

GUERILLA EQUIPMENT
Equipment can be made that works as well as the equipment sold in stores

It is possible to make a video relatively inexpensively. The important thing is to recognize the limitations of your budget and equipment and to successfully work within them. You should never be afraid of the quality of your gear if you are sure of your skills and techniques.

Some equipment companies charge exorbitant amounts of money for basic equipment. Most of the simple tools and material could just as easily be homemade, possibly saving you hundreds of dollars. For example many kinds of camera mounts that indie filmmakers use are homemade. Body mounts, bicycle mounts, and interior and exterior car mounts, for example, can all be made with parts from a home

Wheelchair Dolly

- A great way to do moving shots is through the use of a dolly. But motion picture dollies can cost a lot of money.

- Wheelchairs can make a great dolly, and they are often not too hard to find.

- You can either sit down in the wheelchair and have somebody else push or pull you or mount your camera to the wheelchair itself.

- You can also use skateboards, in-line skates, and baby carriages as dollies; just make sure you shoot on a smooth surface.

Homemade Steadicam

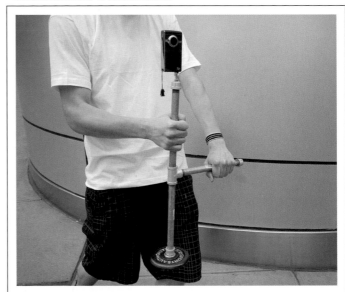

- Steadicams can get you smooth camera movements, but they are very expensive. Even the cheapest Steadicams cost as much as high-end consumer cameras.

- You can build your own Steadicam with $20 worth of parts from your local hardware store and a little bit of handiwork.

improvement store and a little ingenuity. You can make a Steadicam out of a metal or wooden rod and some weights or make a Fig Rig out of PVC piping. A Fig Rig is a camera stabilization device for smaller camcorders designed by film director Mike Figgis. Often, the biggest advantage to making homemade tools is not the savings in money but rather that you can tailor the tools to your specific needs.

Don't feel like you cannot start a film until you have the best equipment. If your only camcorder is a $300 four-year-old standard-definition model, don't let it stop you. Use it. Even the cheapest consumer MiniDV camcorder can give good results when you use a tripod and light properly. Don't feel that you need to rush out and buy a brand new HDV camera, a new boom microphone, or Final Cut Pro. Shoot with the equipment you already own. Learn your equipment and, more importantly, learn the craft of filmmaking.

Work Lights

- Halogen work lamps available from large hardware stores are great for inexpensive lighting.

- They usually draw about 500 watts, and they are nearly daylight-balanced.

- Halogen lights use a lot of power so you must keep an eye on the circuit breaker. They also can get really hot.

- You can bounce the light off of walls or ceilings or use them through an umbrella as you would an actual movie light.

DIY Reflector

- The cheapest possible way to make a useful silver reflector is with cardboard and aluminum foil. You can find these materials at your local supermarket.

- Pick up a large cardboard box and stick the aluminum foil to it. Use the shiny side of the aluminum foil as a hard light reflector and the dull side for a diffused reflector.

- Another inexpensive way to create a reflector is to use a sun shade (an item that is put on a windshield to keep a car cool).

- Remember, anything shiny and silver makes a good reflector.

WEB SITES

Blogs

Cinematical.com
Online blogging and discussion focused on movies, celebrities, and entertainment.

Directorsnotes.com
Directors Notes is a blog and also offers interviews and video podcasts dedicated to independent filmmaking in all its wondrous forms, lengths, and styles.

Filmschoolrejects.com
Delivering movie news, movie reviews, movie trailers, and harsh opinions.

Indiewire.com
Film industry and filmmaker resource for independent and documentary film news, film festivals, and awards.

Indymogul.com
Indy Mogul is the network dedicated to film fanatics and aspiring auteurs alike.

Motionographer.com
A blog community built to showcase and discuss inspiring motion design, motion graphics, animation, visual effects, graphic design, and digital filmmaking.

Slashfilm.com
Blogging the Reel World, movie news, and reviews.
thedocumentaryblog.com
A Web site created by and for documentary fans and filmmakers.

General Sites about Filmmaking

artofthetitle.com
A compendium and leading Web resource of film and television title design from around the world.

Cinematography.com
A must visit for documentary filmmakers. Contains extensive information on all matters relating to cameras and filmmaking.

desktopvideo.about.com
Loads of information for new and seasoned DV filmmakers alike, including buying guides, product reviews, and post-production help.

Film-Makers.com
Online starting point for filmmakers and film lovers. A movie-oriented community site and search engine.

Filmsound.org
Learning space dedicated to the art of film sound design.

Moviemaker.com
Moviemaker is the nation's leading resource on the art and business of making movies and the world's most widely read independent movie magazine.

Screenwriting Web Sites

Creativescreenwriting.com
Magazine Web site for screenwriters and scriptwriters.

Script-o-rama.com
Over 10,000 free movie scripts, transcripts, screenplays, teleplays and more since 1995.

Scriptster.com
Screenwriting evaluation, coverage, and submission services.

SimplyScripts.com
Download the screenplays of hundreds of well-known films, as well as early drafts and sometimes even scans of the original scripts complete with handwritten amendments made during shooting.

Filmmaking Communities and Forums

Creativecow.net
Support communities for digital video, video editing, and media production professionals in broadcasting, motion graphics, and special FX.

Dvinfo.net
The Digital Video Information Network is a technical and creative resource for learning about digital video technology.
DVXuser.com
The online community for filmmaking.
Filmmaking.net
The site provides reference and a community for new and independent filmmakers around the world.
Theauteurs.com
The Auteurs is a social network for people who *love* film.
Withoutabox.com
Withoutabox is a Web site–based film submission service that is a division of the IMDb.

Sites for Movie lovers
AFI.com
AFI is America's promise to preserve the history of the motion picture, educate the next generation of storytellers, and honor the artists and their work.
Apple.com/trailers
The best selection of film trailers and teasers online, many in high definition.
Boxofficemojo.com
BoxOfficeMojo tracks how much films earn at the U.S. and worldwide box office on a daily, weekly, and weekend basis.
Film.com
A great Web site specializing in articles about movies, movie news, actors, and reviews.
Flixster.com
Flixster is a full-featured social network for movie lovers offering film info, reviews, movie trailers, and other media, as well as general social networking features like profiles, comment walls, and friending.
hollywood.com
News on movies and movies in the making.

IMDb.com

No site can match the extensive information that the Internet Movie Database (IMDb) provides its fifty-seven million monthly users. Moviegoers can look up film release dates, watch trailers, and read movie news. But most fans use IMDb to search for films and learn about the cast and crew, nominations and awards, trivia, recommendations, and more.

Netflix.com

Netflix offers online flat-rate DVD and Blu-Ray disc rental-by-mail and video streaming in the United States.

Rottentomatoes.com

Eleven million monthly readers flock to Rotten Tomatoes to read more than 850,000 movie reviews, which are aggregated from various media outlets.

Web Sites for Research and Buying Equipment

bhphotovideo.com

The world's leading retailer of imaging products. The store carries a wide range of products as well as professional and specialty equipment.

Camcorderinfo.com

The #1 site for camcorder reviews.

Cnet.com

Offers reviews of camcorders and cameras as well as other electronics.

Video Sharing Sites

Blip.tv

Rather than focusing on viral sharing and family and friends video hosting, Blip.tv is pointed at Web shows.

RESOURCES

Metacafe.com

This user-generated site specializes in short-form original content. Videos are uploaded by various-sized contributors from independents to major media firms.

Revver.com

Revver splits the ad revenue on all uploads 50/50 with the creator. Users are also able to build their own site based on the Revver API and brand it as their own.

Viddler.com

Another of the most used services, Viddler is known for its advanced technical features.

Vimeo.com

Vimeo has gained a reputation as catering to a high-end, artistic crowd because of its high bit rate, resolution, and HD support.

YouTube.com

Everybody who uses the Internet is familiar with YouTube. The interface is not as nice as Vimeo and it's full of low-quality video, but it is still one of the easiest ways to share your movies with others.

Film Contests

Filmracing.com

Can you make a movie in twenty-four hours?

vidopp.com

Video contest community: new video contests every day for cash or prizes.

youtube.com/contests_main

Section on YouTube where companies post various video contests to win cash and prizes.

48hourfilm.com

Challenges filmmaking teams to produce a movie from scratch in only forty-eight hours.

ADDITIONAL READING

Books on Screenwriting

How Not to Write a Screenplay: 101 Common Mistakes Most Screenwriters Make by Denny Martin Flinn, Lone Eagle, 1999

How to Write a Movie in 21 Days by Viki King, Harper Paperbacks, 1993

Screenplay: The Foundations of Screenwriting by Syd Field, Delta, 2005

The Screenwriter's Bible: A Complete Guide to Writing, Formatting, and Selling Your Script by David Trottier, Silman-James Press, 2005

Story: Substance, Structure, Style and The Principles of Screenwriting by Robert McKee, It Books, 1997

Books on Directing and Cinematography

Directing Actors: Creating Memorable Performances for Film & Television by Judith Weston, Michael Wiese Productions, 1999

Film Directing Shot by Shot: Visualizing from Concept to Screen by Steve Katz, Michael Wiese, 1991

The Five C's of Cinematography: Motion Picture Filming Techniques by Joseph V. Mascelli, Silman-James Press, 1998

Making Movies by Sidney Lumet, Vintage, 1996

On Directing Film by David Mamet, Penguin, 1992

Painting With Light by John Alton, University of California Press, 1995

Books on Editing

Cut by Cut: Editing Your Film or Video by Gael Chandler, Michael Wiese Productions, 2006

The Eye Is Quicker: Film Editing: Making a Good Film Better by Richard D. Pepperman, Michael Wiese Productions, 2004

Film Editing: Great Cuts Every Filmmaker and Movie Lover Must Know by Gael Chandler, Michael Wiese Productions, 2009

In the Blink of an Eye, Revised Second Edition by Walter Murch, Silman-James Press, 2001

The Invisible Cut: How Editors Make Movie Magic by Bobbie O'Steen, Michael Wiese Productions, 2009

Books on Acting

Acting for the Camera, Revised Edition by Tony Barr, Harper Paperbacks, 1997

Acting in Film: An Actor's Take on Movie Making by Michael Caine, Applause Books, 2000

Audition: Everything an Actor Needs to Know to Get the Part by Michael Shurtleff, Walker & Company, 2003

Other Books to Check Out

Easy Riders, Raging Bulls: How the Sex-Drugs-and-Rock 'N' Roll Generation Saved Hollywood by Peter Biskind, Simon & Schuster, 1999

Film School: How to Watch DVDs and Learn Everything about Filmmaking by Richard D. Pepperman, Michael Wiese Productions, 2008

My First Movie: Take Two: Ten Celebrated Directors Talk About Their First Film edited by Stephen Lowenstein, Pantheon, 2008

My First Movie: Twenty Celebrated Directors Talk about Their First Film edited by Stephen Lowenstein, Penguin, 2002

Rebel Without a Crew: Or How a 23-Year-Old Filmmaker With $7,000 Became a Hollywood Player by Robert Rodriguez, Plume, 1996

PHOTO CREDITS

xii (left): © Elena Dremova | Dreamstime.com

xii (right): © Kuznetsov Alexey | Shutterstock

1 (left): © Karin Lau | Dreamstime.com

1 (right): © ixer | Shutterstock

2 (left): © George Grosescu | Dreamstime.com

2 (right): Old Film Reel: © Hannamariah | Shutterstock; Whitetail Peak - Montana: © Jason Maehl | Shutterstock; Blank Brochure: © Albert Campbell | Shutterstock

3 (left): © Roman Guro | Shutterstock

5 (right): © Michal Adamczyk | Dreamstime.com

6 (left): © elsar | Shutterstock

6 (right): © David Coleman | Dreamstime.com

8 (left): © jamie cross | Shutterstock

12 (left): © Deklofenak | Shutterstock

12 (right): © MANDY GODBEHEAR | Shutterstock

13 (left): © Yuri Arcurs | Shutterstock

14: Posters by Lauren Panepinto, www.laurenpanepinto.com

15: Posters by Lauren Panepinto, www.laurenpanepinto.com

17: Posters by Lauren Panepinto, www.laurenpanepinto.com

18 (left): © Brandon Seidel | Dreamstime.com

18 (right): © James Steidl | Dreamstime.com

20 (right): © ArrowStudio, LLC | Shutterstock

21 (right): © James Steidl | Dreamstime.com

24 (left): © Joyce Michaud | Dreamstime.com

27 (left): © Blaz Kure | Shutterstock

28: Posters by Lauren Panepinto, www.laurenpanepinto.com

29: Poster by Lauren Panepinto, www.laurenpanepinto.com

31: Poster by Lauren Panepinto, www.laurenpanepinto.com

42 (right): © Brykaylo Yuriy | Shutterstock

48 (right): © Dom1 | Dreamstime.com

59 (right): Courtesy of Panasonic Corporation

66 (right): © Teslenko Petro | Dreamstime.com

70 (right): © Thomas M Perkins | Shutterstock

71 (left): © D. Kusters | Shutterstock

77 (left): © James M Phelps, Jr | Shutterstock

85 (left): © Sergio Bertino | Dreamstime.com

94 (right): © Snezhok | Dreamstime.com

96 (left): © KK Art and Photography | Shutterstock

103 (left): © Ken Hurst | Shutterstock

106 (right): © Brenda Carson | Shutterstock

107 (left): © Nadina | Shutterstock

127 (left): © Laurin Rinder | Shutterstock

132 (left): © Suzanne Tucker | Shutterstock

133 (left): © Michelle Robek | Dreamstime.com

133 (right): © Gary Paul Lewis | Shutterstock

137 (right): © Jeanne Hatch | Shutterstock

140 (left): © Bowie15 | Dreamstime.com

141 (left): © Noam Armonn | Shutterstock

145 (left): © Alexey Stiop | Shutterstock

148 (left): Photo by Zach Manfredi

152 (right): © aispl | Shutterstock

153 (left): © Kateryna Naumova | Shutterstock

153 (right): © alexwhite | Shutterstock

154 (right): © Nikita Sobolkov | Dreamstime.com

155 (left): © Rochak Shukla | Dreamstime.com

155 (right): © Alex Varlakov | Dreamstime.com

163 (left): © Denis Dryashkin | Dreamstime.com

163 (right): © Robert Latawiec | Dreamstime.com

164 (left): © Cable Risdon

170 (right): Photo by Alex Schwaeber

171 (left): Photo by Alex Schwaeber

171 (right): © Brad Calkins | Dreamstime.com

173 (left): © Skyline | Shutterstock

176 (right): © Pavel Losevsky | Dreamstime.com

180 (left): © Eric Limon | Dreamstime.com

181 (left): © Scorpion26 | Dreamstime.com

182 (right): © Sebastian Kaulitzki | Dreamstime.com

183 (left): © makikSM | Shutterstock

189 (right): Courtesy of Rosco Laboratories, Inc.

198 (right): © Iznogood | Shutterstock

200 (left): © Sandra Sims | Dreamstime.com

200 (right): © R.T. Wohlstadter | Shutterstock

201 (left): © 3DDock | Shutterstock

201 (right): © John Kounadeas | Dreamstime.com

202 (left): Photo by Zach Manfredi

204 (right): © Aaron Kohr | Dreamstime.com

205 (left): © Helder Almeida | Dreamstime.com

206 (left): © rheme | Shutterstock

206 (right): Laptop: © Yuri Arcurs | Shutterstock; Graphic: © Ozger
Aybike Sarikaya | Shutterstock

209 (left): © cobalt88 | Shutterstock

211 (left): © mangostock | Shutterstock

212 (left): Laptop: © Bánhidi Zsolt | Dreamstime.com; Graphic: ©
Ozger Aybike Sarikaya | Shutterstock

212 (right): © Brooke Fuller | Shutterstock

213 (left): © corepics | Shutterstock

215 (left): © Jiri Flogel | Shutterstock

216 (left): © Alex Kalmbach | Shutterstock

216 (right): Poster by Lauren Panepinto, www.laurenpanepinto.com

217 (left): © James Steidl | Shutterstock

217 (right): © iDesign | Shutterstock

220 (left): © Anatoliy Samara | Dreamstime.com

221 (left): © Robert Kyllo | Shutterstock

224 (right): © Lisa F. Young | Shutterstock

226 (left): © Jump Photography | Shutterstock

227 (left): © Glenn Jenkinson | Shutterstock

GLOSSARY

3D: A film that has a three-dimensional, stereoscopic form or appearance, giving the lifelike illusion of depth; often achieved by viewers donning special red/blue (or green) or polarized lens glasses.

5.1 Channel Digital Sound: The digital sound exhibition standard for film, which utilizes five output speaker channels (left, center, right, right surround, left surround, and subwoofer).

24 Frames per Second: Refers to the standard frame rate or film speed, the number of frames or images that are projected or displayed per second.

Above the Line: Refers to the creative elements of a production such as the writer, producer, director, and actors.

Act: A main division within the plot of a film.

ADR: Automatic Dialogue Replacement. Also known as "looping." A process of re-recording dialogue in the studio in synchronization with the picture.

Aliasing: An undesirable distortion component that can arise in any digitally encoded information.

Ambiance: The feeling or mood of a particular scene or setting.

Antagonist: The main character, person, group, society, nature, force, spirit world, bad guy, or villain of a film or script who is in adversarial conflict with the film's hero, lead character, or protagonist.

Anti-Aliasing: Filtering of erroneous frequencies that are created during the analog to digital conversion process.

Aperture: A variable opening inside a lens that regulates the amount of light reaching the image plane. Also known as an iris.

Arthouse: A motion picture theater that shows foreign or non-mainstream independent films.

Aspect Ratio: The proportion of picture width to height (1.33:1, 1.66:1, 1.85:1 or 2.35:1).

Barn Doors: Folding doors which are mounted onto the front of a light unit in order to control illumination.

Beat: Refers to an actor's term for how long to wait before doing an action; a beat is usually about one second.

Blocking: Plotting actor, camera, and microphone placement and movement in a production or scene.

Boom: A telescoping arm for a camera or microphone available in a variety of sizes, from the very small handheld types to the very large.

C47s: Ordinary wooden clothespins that are used to secure gels to barn doors.

CGI: Computer-Generated Imagery (or Images), a term referring to the use of 3D computer graphics and technology (digital computers and specialized software) in filmmaking to create filmed images, special effects, and the illusion of motion; often used to cut down on the cost of hiring extras.

C-Stand: A general-purpose grip stand.

Call Sheet: A form which refers to all of the scenes to be filmed and all of the personnel and equipment required for shooting on a particular day.

Clipping: The phenomenon in which an input signal exceeds the capability of electronic or digital equipment to reproduce the signal.

Codec: A video or audio compression component that can both compress and decompress (encode and decode) files.

Composition: Refers to the arrangement of different elements (i.e., colors, shapes, figures, lines, movement, and lighting) within a frame and in a scene.

Contrast: Refers to the difference between light and shadow, or between maximum and minimum amounts of light, in a particular film image.

Crew: Refers to those involved in the technical production of a film who are not actual performers.

Cutaway: A brief shot that momentarily interrupts a continuously filmed action, by briefly inserting another related action, object, person.

Deinterlace: The motion between interlaced fields can cause visibl tearing when displayed on a computer monitor. Deinterlacing uses every other line from one field and interpolates new in-between lines without tearing. See also interlace, NTSC.

Depth of Field: The amount of space within lens view that will maintain acceptable focus at given settings.

Diegetic (diegesis): Realistic or logically existing, such as the music that plays on a character's radio in a scene; more generally, it refers to the narrative elements of a film (such as spoken dialogue, other sounds, action) that appear in, are shown, or naturally originate within the content of the film frame; the opposite is non-diegetic elements, such as sounds (e.g., background music, the musical score, a voiceover, or other sounds) without an origin within the film frame itself.

Dolly Shot: Any shot made from a moving dolly.

Dub (or dubbing): The act of putting a new soundtrack on a film or adding a soundtrack (of dialogue, sound effects, or music) after production, to match the action of already filmed shots.

Dutch Angle: A camera angle in which the horizontal frame line is not parallel to the horizon.

Epilogue: A short, concluding scene in a film in which characters (sometimes older) reflect on the preceding events.

Equalization: The alteration of sound frequencies for a specific purpose, such as to remove "noise" frequencies or to improve speech clarity.

Eyeline Match: A cut between two shots that creates the illusion of the character (in the first shot) looking at an object (in the second shot).

FireWire: A digital data interface standard that provides a high-speed plug-and-play interface for personal computers. Used for connecting DV camcorders to computers, as well as to hard disk drives and DVD drives. Supports up to 480 Mbps data rate. Also known as IEEE 1394.

Foley: Creating sound effects by watching the picture and mimicking the action, often with props that do not exactly match the action.

Feature Film: A "full-length" motion picture, one greater than 60 minutes in length—but usually about 90–120 minutes.

Fourth Wall: Refers to the imaginary, illusory invisible plane through which the film viewer or audience is thought to look toward the action; the fourth wall that separates the audience from the characters is "broken" when the barrier between the fictional world of the film's story and the "real world" of the audience is shattered—e.g., when an actor speaks directly to the viewers by making an aside.

Gaffer: The chief lighting technician for a production, who is in charge of the electrical department.

Interlaced Video: A technique used for television video formats, such as NTSC and PAL, in which each full frame of video actually consists of alternating lines taken from two separate fields captured at slightly different times.

Jump-Cut: An editorial device by which the action is noticeably advanced in time, either accidentally or for the purpose of creating an effect on the viewer.

Juxtaposition: In a film, the contiguous positioning of either two images, characters, objects, or two scenes in sequence, in order to compare and contrast them, or establish a relationship between them.

Lavalier Mic: A small microphone that can be easily hidden on a piece of clothing so as not to be seen by the camera.

Lossless: Any compression scheme, especially for audio and video data, that uses a nondestructive method that retains all the original information, and therefore does not degrade sound or video quality.

Lossy: Any compression scheme, especially for audio and video data, that removes some of the original information in order to significantly reduce the size of the compressed data.

Master Shot: A continuous shot or long take that shows the main action or setting of an entire scene.

MIDI: Musical Instrument Digital Interface. A machine protocol that allows synthesizers, computers, drum machines, and other processors to communicate with and/or control one another.

Neutral Density (ND): Colorless filters that reduce the amount of light in controlled degrees.

Noise: In audio systems, noise is the electrical interference or other unwanted sound introduced into the system (i.e. hiss, hum, rumble, crosstalk, etc.).

NTSC: National Television Standards Committee. The organization that sets the American broadcast and videotape format standards for the FCC; also refers to the U.S. and Japanese video systems that have 525 horizontal scan lines, 16 million different colors, and 30 frames per second.

Pixel: The individual picture elements, or "dots" of color, that are arranged in a two-dimensional array to define a digital image or video frame.

Production Sound: Recording and/or mixing sound on location during the film or video shoot.

Product Placement: Refers to how companies buy advertising space within a film for their products, as a way for a producer to fund some film production costs.

Progressive Video: Video consisting of complete frames, not interlaced fields.

Reaction Shot: A quick shot that records a character's or group's response to another character or some on-screen action or event.

Reverse Angle: A shot that is turned approximately 180 degrees in relation to the preceding shot.

Room Tone: The "noise" of a room, set, or location where dialogue is recorded during production.

Sepia Tone: A black-and-white image that has been converted to a sepia tone or color (a brownish gray to a dark olive brown) in order to enhance the dramatic effect and/or create an "antique" appearance.

Shotgun Mic: A highly directional microphone, usually with a long, tubular body; used by the production sound mixer on location or on the set for film and television productions.

Slate: The identifier placed in front of the camera at the beginning of a take.

Sound Effect: A recorded or electronically produced sound that matches the visual action taking place on screen.

Speed of Sound: The velocity of sound in air is 770 mi/hr. This speed is influenced by temperature and air pressure however.

Split Screen: An optical or special effects shot in which two separate images are combined on each frame.

Subtext: The deeper and usually unexpressed "real" meanings of a character's spoken lines or actions.

Surround Sound: Sound that is reproduced through speakers above or behind the audience.

Tag Line: A clever phrase or short sentence to memorably characterize a film, tease and attract potential viewers, or sell the movie.

THX: A theatrical film exhibition sound system that maintains a consistent sound standard from theater to theater.

Time Code: A time code is a sequence of numeric codes generated at regular intervals by a timing system. Time codes are used extensively for synchronization, and for logging material in recorded media.

Time Lapse: A method of filming in which frames are shot much slower than their normal rate, allowing action to take place between frames, and giving the appearance of the action taking place much faster in the finished product.

Trailer: A short publicity film, preview, or advertisement composed of short excerpts and scenes from a forthcoming film or coming attraction, usually two to three minutes in length; often presented at the showing of another film.

USB (Universal Serial Bus): A digital data interface standard providing a plug-and-play interface for personal computers. Typically used for lower-speed peripherals such as mice, keyboards, printers, and scanners. Also used for interfacing to digital cameras.

Voiceover: Narration or asynchronous dialogue taking place over the action on screen.

Widescreen: A general term for film presentation in which a film is shown in an aspect ratio of greater than 1.33 to 1.

XLR: One of several varieties of sound connectors having three or more conductors plus an outer shell that shields the connectors and locks the connectors into place.

INDEX

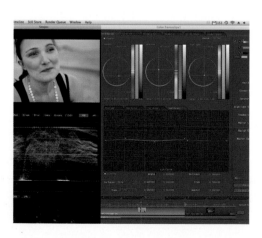

INDEX

INDEX